Praise for *Radi*

"If you're serious about unlo
becoming the best version of yourself, then *Radical Rein-vention* is the book you simply can't afford to overlook. As someone who has personally had to rebuild their reputation and start from scratch, I can tell you that this book speaks to the very heart of transformation. The eight stages presented will demystify the reinvention process and make it feel achievable, while the truly transformative results will leave you stunned. The 'Re-Inventor's Playbook' is packed with gripping stories of real-life Re-Inventors who have successfully transformed their lives, providing irrefutable evidence that it's never too late to start anew."

—TOM HARDIN,
FORMER FBI INFORMANT "TIPPER X"

"With disruption all around us, the pace of change overwhelms us. In *Radical Reinvention*, Maureen Lippe shares the secrets to surviving and thriving by navigating the waters of change. Through her inspiring stories and examples, we can all learn to embrace and master reinvention."

—GREG MORLEY,
GLOBAL HEAD OF DIVERSITY,
EQUITY & INCLUSION, MOËT HENNESSY

"Maureen Lippe has created lightning in a book! She's put it all on the table to take readers through the journey of a lifetime. The pandemic left many searching for their purpose and it is at this moment that Maureen can help readers to radically reinvent themselves. This is the moment to step into courage and take an adventure of a lifetime."

—HOLLAND HAIIS, LEADERSHIP CONSULTANT, SPEAKER,
AND AWARD-WINNING AUTHOR

"*Radical Reinvention* is the life-changing guide we have all been begging for without even realizing it! Maureen does a knockout job at explaining why each of us should welcome reinvention as an organic, ever evolving entity within our very beings. Not only is *Radical Reinvention* a healing process and survival tactic; Maureen also discusses why we owe it to ourselves to look deep within our very souls, expand outside our contrived boundaries and literally create beauty from chaos."

—MANDI CHAMBLESS,
14-YEAR STAGE IIIC OVARIAN CANCER SURVIVOR AND
THRIVING RE-INVENTOR

"*Radical Reinvention* is a must read for everyone who wants to improve themselves. It describes 8 stages everyone must go through to achieve success through this process. Maureen Lippe goes beyond personal experience and includes many personal stories of others, supported by the experience of industry experts. Our only suggestion to those raising dual-career families is that they don't try to reinvent both partners at the same time!"

—ILENE GORDON AND BRAM BLUESTEIN, CO-AUTHORS, DOUBLING DOWN: THE SECRET SAUCE FOR DUAL CAREER FAMILIES

"This is a book you will pick up and not be able to put down until it's finished. Never have we had a time in our lives that *Radical Reinvention* was more needed. This is an action that we must demand of ourselves. We must be courageous in calling out what we no longer can allow to remain silent within us, and in so doing, we create the future that we have longed to have. If you ever thought you were alone and no one saw you, know that after reading this book you will walk away with the tools to stand and face who you are truly purported to be. Be unapologetic in embracing your purpose! Life is too short. The world needs your voice, now."

—DONNA M. WILSON, PRESIDENT OF STRATEGIC INTERSECTIONS LLC, GLOBAL DIVERSITY, EQUITY, AND INCLUSION EXECUTIVE

"An exciting and educational glimpse behind the scenes of *Vogue* and career building in the world of fashion, as well as an inclusive and interesting exploration of reinvention, through various perspectives with helpful resources from experts like Idea Whisperer Mitch Markson, author of *The Imagination Playbook*."

—*Jazz Biancci,*
Author, Speaker, Conscientious Advisor

RADICAL REINVENTION

REIMAGINE, RESET, REINVENT
IN A DISRUPTIVE WORLD

MAUREEN LIPPE

I so passionately dedicate this book to my glorious husband, Jerry Taylor, my love and life sharer who taught me so much about living with joy, passion, and purpose. He mentored me on business skills and how to sell to win—all helping me succeed in life and business. And to my wonderful and irreplaceable son, Nick, my true loyalist who worked so closely with me editing my life and this book.

Our Wedding, 1983.

CONTENTS

ACKNOWLEDGMENTS

I would never have opened up my heart and my hurt to write this deeply personal book if it wasn't for my beautiful husband whose passing tore my heart out and sent me on the painful journey to find myself again and come back from the depths not just surviving but thriving. I'm not totally there yet, but I've learned and felt so much. I have desire and purpose to share my journey and how I became strong again, conquering the fear and the loneliness with wisdom, strength, and peace—and to being committed to never losing myself, my joy and wonder again.

I'm profoundly grateful to Candi Cross, who called me up one day and said you've come a long way on this journey of many meaningless days and nights feeling broken and lost; you need to write a book on how you're reinventing yourself and your company all at the same time, let's do it together. Her Southern charm, humor and talent kept me going as she tirelessly encouraged me to keep moving forward and never give up on the project and my promise to help myself and others who are suffering. Her commitment and dedication to getting this book to press was relentless. She became my therapist, my friend and was gentle during the periods when I just couldn't concentrate on this project. I deeply thank her for her patience with me and her deep talent. She worked tirelessly finding great "Re-Inventors" to share their courageous stories. Candi's unflagging support in every aspect of this book with such enthusiasm and hard work kept me motivated and made this book possible.

My deep gratitude goes to Nick Taylor for his help in supporting me through this process, plus helping to edit this book, including constantly encouraging me to go deeper, put it all out there and add more of my very personal experiences. He stressed for me to do it with the humor that he says embodies who I am and what helped me get through without anger or bitterness. "Just be your authentic self, Mom."

To my friend and business partner, Paul Dyer—this is for you. Thank you for the support you offered me during the many lost months. I owe much of my recovery to you. Never did you pressure me after Jerry's death to perform any more than I was capable of at the time. You were an authentic partner embodying leadership with empathy and caring. Your encouragement to write a book is what made me do it. I'm grateful to the compassion and counsel you offered me during the difficult times. Not only did you help with my personal reinvention, but also, the reinvention of Lippe Taylor. You are the best partner and friend a girl could ask for. Thank you.

To all my friends and colleagues at Lippe Taylor, you were my lifeline. Seeing you every week and just feeling the love warmed my heart and healed my hurt. I will be eternally grateful. We were all suffering together during and post-COVID-19. We survived, and many of us are thriving again as friends and leaders. I love you all.

A sincere thank you to the many clients who I've had the privilege to serve over the last 30 years. You were the bloodline of the agency and the conduit to Lippe Taylor's success. You made us better every day. You were the change agents of the future and a motivation for this book.

To my darling Remy, who is my nanny, bodyguard, healer, and wonderful friend. You saved me. I will never forget. I love you so deeply. A big thanks to Kay for the love and sharing of her mom all these years.

To all my loving family and friends, you brought me closer to sanity every day. I am forever grateful. Thank you.

Finally, a note of thanks to our Re-Inventors: I am so indebted to all the courageous, brazen fire starters who so authentically opened their wounds in telling their stories of how they took their lives back after setbacks and major obstacles that railroaded their life and careers. And to all who shared their brave business reinventions. So many examples of authentic, modern leadership. They are all fearless leaders who navigated uncharted life and business circumstances and flourished as stronger versions of themselves. I respect you so much and thank you for gracing my book with your brave journeys. Your stories and strategies inspired me: Samantha Lux, Irene Brank, Eric Alva, Fern Mallis, Alina Lee, Craig Stanland, Liz G. Bailey, Halena Cline, Barri Rafferty, Carlos Zepeda, Dr. Nadya Zhexembayeva, Weatherly Camacho, Dr. Ann Turner, Liza Andrews, Keiya Rayne, Irina Soriano, Nick Taylor, and Paul Dyer. Thank you.

re-

back, back from, back to the original
place; undoing; again, ANEW

In the world of *Radical Reinvention*, second chances entice
you to roll the dice again. Look closely this time. Savor
the possibilities. **Rediscover, realign, recharge, rebuild,
realign, recover,** and **rebrand** for a more splendid you.
It's all within your grasp, your nature. Be unapologetic.
Embrace the future you have longed for most of your life.
Never has there been a more perfect time for reinvention.
The world needs your voice and power now. It takes brave
work. Nobody said it would be easy. Have the courage to
develop your potential and your purpose. Put your whole
heart into it and let's rise strong together.

SURVIVE OR THRIVE NOW

"For me, 'revolution' simply means radical change."

—*Aung San Suu Kyi, activist*

THE STEADY, CLASSIC turtle isn't exactly known for its swagger, but its reinvention as a species has endured for about 90 million years. Respect! Turtles have been around longer than dinosaurs. They survived the asteroid that crashed into the Yucatán that killed the dinosaurs 86 million years ago. It's probably because they were still buried in the ground. When they came up, it was dark and cold, but they could live. Scientists from the Smithsonian recently traced back the inception of its shell: ribs and spine, which grew steadily thicker before eventually fusing together to form an exterior shell made up of about fifty pieces—all to adopt new ways of breathing and moving from its complex structure. A beacon of persistence, survival, and reinvention. They can easily retract into their shell for long periods of time. That is exactly what we do when we're in dark places hurting or in danger; we retract into our shells when life gets hard. That is exactly what we don't want you to do and why I wrote this book to prevent that from happening to you and to me. The oldest living tortoise, Jonathan, just turned 190 years old. He is also the oldest known living land animal. Let that set in. Talk about *resilience*!

And what about you? Have you retracted? Are you now ready to take risks? Do you need to reinvent to survive? To break out of a miserable, painful, traumatic setback, loss, or failure? To breathe again? To test your courage and rise? To explore the full spectrum of your potential? To build an abundant life after losing it all to rebuild magnificent you? To make the rest of your life the best you could imagine? A personal brand that sustains, never retracts?

Alongside the wondrous animal planet in constant regeneration, people are ascending the scale of regeneration to *radical reinvention*. Chances are, this is *you*. The planet is exploding with brave reinventions. Radical Re-Inventors are the fire starters, casting the sparkling flames above the rest. They are not only rebranding their minds but often, their bodies. They are setting humanity's table with abundant fruits of ingenuity, empathy, truth, excitement, and rising stronger than ever.

Drastic Disruption Calls for Radical Reinvention

In *The Pandemic Is a Portal*, author Arundhati Roy writes, "Historically, pandemics have forced humans to break with the past and imagine their world anew. This one is no different. It is a portal, a gateway between one world and the next."

Thank you, Arundhati, we'll surely be imagining and reimagining soon! First, let's reflect a bit, as what we've gone through is unmatched in our lifetime. My God, how did we all get through this period? Did we? We need to Review (see Chapter 1) the experiences, the emotions inside of us, the fear and uncertainty to understand what we're working with to begin our Radical Reinvention odysseys.

Pandemics disrupt civilizations. Now, you and I know firsthand! We must Radically Reinvent despite what the catalyst is though. This moment is the time for reset and thinking about how to reinvent, then realizing that prized vision with deliberate actions. We're all in this together and we've got to get through it. Self-care has never been more important. Mental wellness and loneliness are world dialogue right now and it should be because of COVID-19 and what this radical era has dumped on us.

At the same time, we can't ignore other great catalysts for change. My life blew up on steroids because my life as I knew and loved it was swept away from me due to the loss of my big love of almost forty years, Jerry Taylor, causing terror, uncertainty, and painful loss. I had to try hard to reclaim my identity and become a whole human again. Miraculously, over time, I created a toolkit of what really helped me—with many emotional moments and resonance that it could help others; thus, this book.

I knew serial reinvention and even welcomed it, enduring the growing pains and embracing the new features. This was my life, but then horrible things happened in the last few years that violated my existence and forced me to look inside. I had to reconcile existence without my husband, my love and partner for so many glorious years.

Previous reinventions were never spun out of profound loss and grief. The bigger reinventions were never without my loving partner by my side.

To be fully transparent, I was always able to elevate my personal brand, as well as the brands of my clients, but now, I had to build a new life despite fear, loneliness, and uncertainty. I had to lead from my heart, not my hurt. It took brave work and hard conversations with myself. These are not merely words.

Whether you also lost your greatest love, fell ill, a mind-blowing technology upended your product or brand, or you have a marvelous dream of your future self unprovoked by a tragedy (and good for you!), I want you to consider following the path to peace, serenity, love, and safety again. I passionately want to help you become whole again. I will hold your hand, guiding you through my journey and what brought me back.

Get ready because I'm going under the knife, revealing raw tissue, muscle, and heart to share these learnings with you. It's makeover time, and it may even get a little bloody. Sometimes they do. We don't need to grow a shell like the radically resilient turtle to reveal the anatomy of Radical Reinvention. It can be a slaughterhouse of emotions to paint the picture. However, Francis Bacon said, "The best part of beauty is that which no picture can express."

Reinvention is a fundamental part of me, as well as my personal brand. I believe in the power of makeovers, whether a redo of our entire life or one specific area, whenever we desire. In fact, makeovers are the gateway to reinvention. Who doesn't love a great makeover?

After leaving my editorial positions at *Vogue* magazine and *Harper's Bazaar* to launch my own consulting firm and then PR agency, I was a spokesperson for Clairol, and their biggest PR challenge was getting on Regis Philbin's show. I wrote a segment idea, which their PR department pitched, and they accepted. When I got on the air, Regis launched into, "This is Maureen Lippe, former beauty editor...*former?* I thought you were the beauty editor of *Harper's Bazaar.*" He chuckled in his hearty way. We had this banter back and forth, and I called him a "low-life creep" on the air! An irreverent moment, but apparently, my sarcasm scored points. Two New Yorkers having some fun with each other. His producer asked me if I wanted to do something permanently for the show: I said yes, makeovers. I had already been doing makeovers in the magazines and now on TV for the last two years. I was the 'makeover queen.' I landed a weekly Friday spot, which would eventually optimize my impact and set my PR agency up for success in fashion, beauty, wellness, and health sectors, as we did beauty/wellness segments on Regis. That never would have happened if I hadn't had the confidence to come back at Regis with humor when he hit me with "you're the former beauty editor." Humor works and it's a big part of my success DNA both personally and professionally. Then I appeared on Charlie Rose and Maury Povich's daytime shows. I loved these two because they intellectualized the discussion of reinvention through makeover. They fully understood the power. I loved doing full-body makeovers on women and men all over the country for one reason: the transformation I saw from all those who were made over both inside and out. Some of their reinventions were simply life changing, and it was only the beginning—physical transformation. I could see in their eyes the spark to thrive. The thrill of a personal makeover or reinvention was life changing. As one woman said to me after her head-to-toe makeover, "I never knew I was beautiful."

Surviving or thriving is a decision to be made in this moment. What is going on? What is giving you anxiety? What is breaking your heart? As you discover and disclose information, if you lead people or an entire brand, reconcile that so much of what we talk about regarding personal development and home life applies to leadership also. Leadership is not for the office only; it's everywhere, it should permeate your life if you're brave enough. You must have internal power wherever you work and inside your home, too, with your spouse and family including your pets. People are not talking about it as much because it may have been construed as too private or too vulnerable. What happens inside will happen outside. But if you cultivate the skills for outside, it will also work inside.

Reinvention is a road. Radical Reinvention is a rough road that opens to a major highway to majestic destinations. It's painful. It cries for courage. It's illuminating. Sometimes construction locks the brakes for a while before you see the new, shiny reconstruction. You must reinvent with what you have. Avoidance is the internal dialogue, *I don't want to go there.* Avoidance is comfort with no courage. Not thinking, not feeling, certainly not acting. I have experienced all of this. And giving in is merely survival. Stepping out is thriving.

When is it time to reinvent? A series of setbacks and obstacles leading to a lot of confusion, forced action, and meaningless days and relationships have railroaded your life. Perhaps you were complacent, satisfied but not fulfilled. It takes Radical Reinvention to better position yourself for opportunities. You have to fight through, take responsibility, be vulnerable, do the reset and come out swinging in this Radically Reinvented world. Loving ourselves during this process of owning our personal story is possibly the bravest thing we will ever do.

And brands...wow, look at you! Amazon, Netflix, Zoom, Door Dash, TikTok, YouTube, but the new kids are brands like Etsy, Ford Motor Co. with the F150 Lightning, Disney winning the streaming wars, brands like Gushers using TikTok to return from obscurity to being hot... and how about all the innovation of AI and ChatGPT, and all the rest to follow? So exciting! These are only a handful of the darlings of the corporate arena and the new upstarts that are Radically Reinventing with technology, innovation, and imagination. My company, Lippe Taylor, certainly had to reinvent to survive. We had to dive in headfirst to survive. Thousands of small businesses, hundreds of nonprofits, underwent rebranding. Some made it; many didn't. It was hard work.

What your personal Radical Reinvention is must be explored inside-out. But you're already living radically now, being forced to change behavior, health, family, and home patterns—all uniquely human. No matter where you are on the spectrum of change, the environment you once operated in, the people in your life have radically shifted with the pandemic of coronavirus, COVID-19. For brands, service and product array, dissemination, consumer base, messaging, mission, and even the very creation of personal brands may have altered. Teams engaged differently. Many of these teams disbanded. Leaders responded by recalibrating their approach toward employees, seeing—authentically *seeing*—them as whole individuals, and infusing purpose in their missions. My own longstanding values as a leader—vision, empathy, trust, accountability, authenticity, empowerment of others, taking a results-oriented approach without a frantic sense of urgency—elevated during this difficult time because of my concern for my staff of more than 250 marvelous human beings at Lippe Taylor. While professional, my affection and care for our people was unconditional. I refused to lose any of them from the company, at least not due to my own shortcomings as their leader, and while they were experiencing their own fears and loss, no doubt. Win or lose together, no other way in my world. It took courage. It took brave work, care, and connection with our people. It was hard and it was scary, but the leadership, our CEO and brilliant teams were all great allies, helping every step of the way.

All this disruption and disorientation got me to thinking about the tenants of this book and the components of reinvention: feeling, processing, reimagining, resetting, and doing. Bravely living and ready to recover. Getting that spark of inspiration that won't burn out upon the first obstacle, distraction, or worse, demon—an illogical element that attempts to scare us from reinventing (see Chapter 6). Under the work tent, there's also what I have coined "bleedership". Wow, some bloodsucking leaders will drain you dry! No empathy, courage or even connection with their people. How do we start to develop braver, more daring, caring, and courageous leaders?

In case you can't already tell, this is not a conventional self-help book about mere change. Change is constant. Change is hard. Why do status quo? It's in my inherent curiosity and authentic nature to take risks, push limits, and try to live fearlessly. It was difficult these last two years to live authentically. It was a struggle for me. These traits serve a Radical Re-Inventor, but it was painful for me much of the time. These traits take courage and are empowering. I don't say that lightly because every board and brand I've been involved with has centered on women's equity and empowerment particularly in under-served communities. I've reinvented many times, and I have learned so much from every round. We must have the pure courage to fully develop our potential and it can get messy.

One thing I know for sure is, though it's not something you feel and think every day; reinvention is in your human nature. The reason for embarking on the reinvention and results are radical, as mine was, but the way you get there is in stages that are sometimes unpredictable, uncontrollable at first but imperative to develop your potential and live authentic lives. Those 8 stages are:

1. *Review*
2. *Recover*
3. *Reawaken*
4. *Remember*
5. *Reimagine*
6. *Reach*
7. *Replenish*
8. *Rebrand*

As further proof, I have help from friends who are Radical Re-Inventors spilling it all in the "Re-Inventor's Playbook" at the end of each chapter. You will not be the same after you read about these courageous, brazen people, like Samantha Lux, who Radically Reinvented her body to affirm her gender, with her mother, Irene Brank, who guides others to the radical resources they need for affirmation; Eric Alva, who served in the Marines and helped to reinvent human rights in America after losing his leg in the Iraq War; Fern Mallis, who reinvented the entire fashion industry; Alina Lee, teen golf star-turned lawyer and activist reinventing how lawyers treat their clients; Craig Stanland, who made it his business to help people reinvent after he served two years in a federal prison and lost it all; Liz G. Bailey, who fled her abuser to start over with her two kids, reinventing herself to teach the signs of domestic violence and speak out loud for other survivors to leave; and Halena Cline, whose paintings and sculptures grace galleries, museums and private collections worldwide only after she released her mind, body and spirit from an infamous cult obsessed with Armageddon, a place where personal reinvention—not to mention, invention—is forbidden.

These individuals represent their personal brands as fiercely as the companies we discuss, like Lippe Taylor, LVMH (Louis Vuitton Moët Hennessey), and Wells Fargo. We've got brand transformation experts like Barri Rafferty, one of the top women in PR and communications; Carlos Zepeda, who says he has the "reinvention gene", an energy he applies to every second of his life; Chief Reinvention Scientist Dr. Nadya Zhexembayeva, who has helped thousands of leaders reinvent; the best therapists helping us to recover and reset, Weatherly Camacho, LPC, MAC, and Dr. Ann Turner; self-development coach, Liza Andrews, who founded the PictureCure® Methods for reinvention; Keiya Rayne, intuitive healer, success coach and transformational speaker whose own reinvention was nothing short of an earthquake; and all-out branding innovator Irina Soriano, who advocates that personal brand and company brand are cojoined inside "life-brand" and shows us how to understand it and maximize it. I'm thrilled to include my son, Nick Taylor, who has been my reinvention sidekick lifting me up with love and inspiration, plus Lippe Taylor's CEO Paul Dyer, our fearless leader, who speaks about our company and our client and staff reinventions with full transparency and candor.

If you've gone through anything like I have, you feel me, and I feel you. Let's get on with it together. We know it's not easy and takes a lot of strength. So, let's feel, even fall together if we must. Just remember that you are not freakishly alone, even in the scary places that may be simultaneously beckoning you and throwing up a locked, black door. This is how change, trauma, fear, and loss can show up. Just remember that you must reinvent before you lose yourself. Through Radical Reinvention, you will know that the inner strength you can summon is powerful like the regenerating turtle. Somehow, they understand it. So must we.

—*Maureen Lippe*

CHAPTER 1

REVIEW

"Out of suffering have emerged the strongest souls;
the most massive characters are seared with scars."

—KHALIL GIBRAN,

AUTHOR AND PROFESSOR

Stage 1 of Your Radical Reinvention—REVIEW

Resolution and Recommendations for:

Loss | Grief | Devastation | Change |
Contemplation | Acceptance

WHAT HAPPENED TO you? Where are you now? Do you
even know? If you've been spacing out or fogging up lately,
you're not alone. But it's time to come clean with courage
and vulnerability. I won't say anything like "snap out of it"
because that's harsh on an already fragile, vulnerable mind
and body. Cue to the yoga instructor's soothing voice.

"Feel the waves of your breath, sensate the movement of breath beneath your heart center, through your nose… elongate the breath waves…feel your fingers, toes and gently move…gradually surface from your depth. Open your eyes." …All right, skip the rest if you're not the type, but do *open your eyes* and open your whole heart and let's heal together with no shame or blame.

To reimagine, you need a full *review* of what's going on first. Know where you are. Have the courage to reassess your life journey to discover how to transform your future from one of disappointment into an opportunity for progress. So, what do you do when you want to change goals and shift gears? How do you honor your own grief? Trust me. We'll get there together. Let's put one foot in front of the other. Our lives are continuing and we're going to be a part of it. It's a new and different normal. People are resetting in droves, figuring out what their lives really are and what they're not getting, not doing, not feeling. Never have we experienced a time like this when Radical Reinvention was so necessary.

Review of the Big Picture

The International Monetary Fund asserts that COVID-19 changed the world with a shift in behavior, the economy, medicine even how we communicate, care for others, and educate our children. And of course, the digital economy, with the rise of digital behavior such as remote working and learning, telemedicine, delivery services and now AI. The future of work has arrived faster, along with its challenges—many of them potentially multiplied—such as income polarization, worker vulnerability, health equity, more gig work, and the need for workers to adapt to occupational transitions.

Brookings sums it up perfectly: Many, including myself, contracted the virus, and some for the dreadful long haul of symptoms and uncertainty of how our bodies will react in the future from the virus and the vaccine. Americans alone lost over 1 million loved ones and more than 104 million contracted the virus, and still counting. Many lost their jobs and often, their employer-sponsored healthcare. Approximately 31.6 million people had to go to work to provide the rest of us with frontline services, while others worked from home. Schools converted to online instruction. Parents struggled to juggle childcare and work. First responders and medical care providers worked overtime in the most hopeless context to save the lives that they could save with brave empathy. In the end, we lost close to 7 million people worldwide as of March 2023, and we're still losing people.

Are you one of the millions who took part in the Great Resignation? According to the Bureau of Labor Statistics, the number of Americans quitting their jobs hit a record high 4.5 million in November 2021. The hardest-hit sector has been the hospitality industry, followed by entertainment, retail and health services. Major strikes have also taken place across the country, with workers demanding higher pay and better working conditions. COVID-19 seems to have shifted the balance of power between American employers and workers.

Others are not happy with themselves, and blame it on their jobs, relationships, cities. Sometimes it's in your head. You must work on yourself with intention bringing a sense of meaning and purpose to your life. If that inner voice is poking at you, something is misaligned. Only you can identify what that is. Only you can realign. The sooner you are aware, the sooner you hit the road with your emotional belongings. These belongings may only be the mental material of a disruption.

Or could grief be the connecting factor to your Radical Reinvention? This certainly is mine.

My Review

It had to happen when I lost my husband, my person, my everything. I had to embrace my fears, faults, and uncertainties. I had to confront the painful truths before I could begin to find the courage and confidence to heal and lead a more secure, meaningful life. And be sure, pain is part of the process. I disintegrated. I was exhausted and drained. I came to the realization that I had to reinvent, and only a Radical Reinvention would save me.

As of this writing, I'm so much better, happier, and more secure, but my new self-invention is still taking shape. That's a process. The horrifying grief is behind me but sneaks up when I least expect it. It was a terrifying process in which tough questions needed to be addressed. How do I move forward bravely when I'm living with fear, loneliness, and uncertainty? Who am I? How do I rise strong? I've learned a lot. Learning is growth.

My exuberant, loving husband, Jerry Taylor, was a COVID-19 long hauler who had recently been diagnosed with diabetes and AFIB (atrial fibrillation, the most common type of treated heart arrhythmia). He never felt these conditions. He worked every day and operated with youthful energy until COVID-19 scooped us both up and never planted us back down on our solid ground. How would we survive when we were both so sick at the same time and when doctors knew nothing about COVID-19 or how to diagnose or treat us? There wasn't even a test. We were treated for bronchitis in those early weeks. We were both empty.

Jerry and I had long-term care insurance, so I was so fortunate to be able to bring in a beautiful Jamaican soul by the name of Heather, to help us navigate my husband's every physical and medical need. Heather was sent from the gods. They both went for walks, and in a short period of time, they knew everything about each other. I took video and many photographs of them together just walking and sharing secrets. Their friendship was like a tender movie and was a gift to the entire family. My husband had a secret garden of lilies that he had planted for me years ago. She took video of him talking about how much he loved me while he was cutting and tending to his flowers on unsteady feet. What a long-lasting video treasure for me to discover over and over from season to season. It's the little things that mean so much when you're longing for someone you lost. In some ways, you have to honor your grief.

A favorite cemetery is located not far from our house, which we would visit frequently when walking. I would visit my departed friends and say hello to them and observe the beautiful headstones, marveling at the symbols chosen to represent the families and remember the lives of those no longer on this earth. Yet I never thought death would encroach upon my life with my husband anytime soon. This is the fairy tale of love, our sweet love. In the hours you live, laugh, play, and even work with the person you love, as we did, why contemplate a finality that slices you and leaves searing pain and loneliness that could bring you to your knees? Why would you ever go there in your mind?

Soon after the diagnosis of the virus, Jerry became tired a lot of the time. Total fatigue soon took over. I, too, was struggling with the effects of COVID-19 to the point that I couldn't make it upstairs sometimes. We had the early devastating March 2020 strain. My poor lungs were struggling so hard. To see the doctor, it would take me an hour to get dressed. Put my pants on, back to bed. Put on a sweater, back to bed. Sit up to take a phone call or at least try to work, back to bed. As a couple, we went through this dreadful routine every day for weeks and then months, in the case of my darling husband. When I thought we might be out of it together, I lost him.

We had worked and driven home together for over a decade. To have that piece to your life puzzle be removed is devastating. It's a gargantuan shift because he is gone forever; I will never see him again or feel his hand in mine. You are so alone and so vulnerable like never before. I lost my life charge. When we were together, my heart was at peace. You make all your decisions alone now. There's nobody there when you go to bed or when you wake up. Empty space all around you. Who are you going to talk to about well, everything? Forty years of being so much in love and so close and in one day, they are gone forever. How do you come back? You never "get over it"—you just hope you get a bit more used to it each day. How could we possibly make the last part of our life the best part now?

Jerry knew he was dying, and he told me he was dying only hours before he passed. I held his hand, told him of my forever love not knowing that he meant he was dying that night. He wasn't in pain. He was so handsome. It was so peaceful, so final. I can respect all the gifts I received inside his illness, dying and death; it could have been so much worse, but how could I ever live bravely again? I felt no connection to my body or mind. Our family lived together under one roof for more than a year during COVID-19, loving and laughing and desperately trying to heal my husband. We all tried so hard, but we couldn't take him to a hospital for fear of picking up the virus once again and eventually could only do Zoom doctor visits.

Grave loss is excruciating. Would I survive or would I surrender?

A rude awakening was when I went to a doctor's appointment after my husband's death. I still checked 'married.' I couldn't accept checking "single" on the forms. It was too soon. Who was I? Who did I identify with? How would I move forward during this most unpredictable and uncontrollable time? My center was off. I went from living my life as a married woman for all those years to being a widow, no longer married and a single woman alone. Titles that are hard to comprehend. I knew I had to build something around my total devastation. I was devoid of life. These markers of identity are the mundane reminders that you need to reshape components of your identity. Even if you don't participate and control the rebrand of you, it will happen anyway. Why not reframe it yourself?

Reinvention works like time. Even if you refuse to pay attention to the clock, the hours pass. And how not to lose your identity while trying to find your reinvention is important.

The mundane occurrences of your life are reminders that bring you to a place of *acceptance*. Erasing the checkmark next to "married", looking for parking on the busy streets of New York City in the coldest winter of my life, having my meals alone and my life alone, I realized that it was time to reinvent myself again. I had to accept that I lost a life partner, a love partner, a family partner, and even a business partner. As the serial re-inventor, instinctually, I knew I had to grow through my sorrow, not just accept it. I needed to make the last chapters of my life filled with purpose and ever so meaningful. Rise and shine. Time to move on.

Sometimes you want to reinvent. Desire seduces. New territory feels exhilarating when it's a *choice*. But death is radical, so reinvention comes from a radical place. It's a call to your courage.

Very fortunately, I am well-adjusted and grounded, gifts my parents gave to me. Knowing these strengths was part of my review. Months into this adjustment, I realized that I was no longer fixated on trauma and grief, but loss was all around me. I know people who lost their spouses in the last few years, and they are dysfunctional coping with their grief through alcohol and drugs, burning through weeks in bed brushing off their basic responsibilities. They are barely surviving but uniquely human. They have allowed grief to overwhelm and identify them.

Growth or going down a dark road is your choice. The

guiding force for me is my wonderful son, Nick Taylor, and my great friends and family. Also, I go to work and that is my lifeline to the reality of getting up and getting out with purpose and service. Work is transformative for me and keeps me on the straight and narrow. My colleagues in the office gave me the strength I needed those first months with their tender hearts and humanity. My son's nanny, Remy, is now my nanny, best friend, and bodyguard! She rarely left my side. Nick and Remy are the secret sauce of my survival. And Lippe Taylor gives me the courage to keep developing my potential. Deep gratitude for all the wonderful people and things in your life is foundational to the review.

During the early stages of my loss, I interviewed a therapist who instructed me to "punch a pillow and scream in the shower daily and set up an altar with candles and photographs of my husband." Are you kidding me? That's not who I am. I am very lonely for my Jerry Taylor, but I'm not angry. How would she know, however, when she didn't take the time to get to know me and what I personally needed as an individual woman, mother, business owner? Being the curious and diplomatic person I think I am, I gave her the benefit of the doubt—for a moment—and pictured me going to battle with a pillow! At least it gave me a good laugh. Laughter is restorative, and I try to laugh a lot every day. The wild image in my mind, crazed, bed-headed and furious, reminded me of a scene from a Lifetime movie. But in truth, I was never angry, so I didn't have the energy to feed the fantasy of an angry widow. How could I be angry at this beautiful man who contracted COVID-19 and couldn't get out of it? We disconnected from the reality of COVID-19. I was so fortunate for everything we had together. That was never lost on me; I was grateful for everything we shared and tried to remain in that state of constant gratitude. Sometimes it worked and sometimes it didn't. I felt sad, grief-stricken, messed up, but never angry. We were together living, loving and working for all those years. Is there life after big loss? Is there anything left?

Perform the Self-Exam, Dammit!

This very reflection is *review*, coming to terms with the full breadth of experience and emotions. Without it, you float or wallow with no anchor, and you might find yourself in oblivion. You pay attention to nothing. If you don't perform a review, an assessment of what occurred, along with your current circumstances, the lack of concrete data in your heart and brain is dangerous, causing an explosion of consequences that may set you back twice as far as the actual event. Judgment is impaired. There is no clarity. Some decisions can't wait. It's all overwhelming filled with uncertainty, but you must ask yourself who you want to now be. The review is the beginning of the journey to survival; it is unpredictable and uncontrollable at first. It takes brave work.

For example, that November and December after Jerry died, the family celebrated Thanksgiving, my birthday, my anniversary plus Christmas and New Year's—all the 'firsts' without my person, my partner. It was heart-crushing. I had to get through the 'firsts' not only for me but also, for my family. I thought, if I get through it, so will my son and his wife, Holly, Julie, Scott, Marianne, Remy, Kay, and our grandchildren. We were all in it together and we wanted to feel the joy of each occasion. I also tried to do it courageously for my husband. I wanted him to be proud of me. If you experienced such great loss, too, crossing the doorframe of the grand, emotional 'firsts' where memories and yearnings will taunt you the most, you'll know what I mean. It's an extreme challenge. Missing him became part of remembering him. It was a way of keeping him alive in my mind and my heart.

Death is not an ending; I try to keep my husband very present in my memory. I hope to hold him within me. But how do you overcome the darkness? The heaviness of grief? The level of pain you never experienced before? There is no precedent for radical loss. It takes strength to process everything. Think of it as tinder for the fire of your reinvention. You'll need a lot of it.

Many people look for 'closure' after a loss without accepting all the parts. In his book, *Finding Meaning*, David Kessler argues that it's finding meaning beyond the stages of grief most of us are familiar with—denial, anger, bargaining, depression, and acceptance—that can transform grief into a more peaceful and hopeful experience. Kessler provides a roadmap to remembering those who have died with more love than pain; he shows us how to move forward in a way that honors our loved ones. Kessler's insight is both professional and intensely personal. His journey with grief began when, as a child, he witnessed a mass shooting at the same time his mother was dying. For most of his life, Kessler taught physicians, nurses, counselors, police, and first responders about end of life, trauma, and grief, as well as leading talks and retreats for those experiencing grief. Despite his knowledge, his life was upended by the sudden death of his twenty-one-year-old son. How does the grief expert handle such a tragic loss? He knew he had to find a way through this unexpected, devastating loss, a way that would honor his son. That, ultimately, was the sixth state of grief—*meaning*. "Meaning appears in the small moments. Name the moment. Find a way to connect," Kessler recommends.

I can relate to all this. At the same time, being imperfect human beings means that awareness is progress, but there are setbacks in the process. My heart started to race a little bit as I was learning about all the different stages that I have not gone through. I don't harp on the negative. When my husband was sick, I didn't feel sorry for myself or fixate on fear. I kept living in the moment with him, trying to make him happy, listening to his music, watching "Grace and Frankie", on all…the…time. I could recite all the dialogue. It gave him comfort. Our family household accepted that show would be on day and night. I still hear the lines from the show, see me and Jerry holding hands and smiling together. I have not been able to watch the show again since his death. I love Jane Fonda and Lily Tomlin, but enough is enough.

One day, I met Sharon, a good friend and former assistant when I worked at *Harper's Bazaar*. She was by my side when I met Jerry and when I fell so deeply in love with him and just so hard and so fast. I couldn't work. I couldn't sleep. I would just pine for our moments together. It was painful but pure bliss when we were together. Not very liberated, just totally in deep love. I recently showed

Sharon photographs. We talked about Jerry's life. I allowed myself to talk about how much I missed him, and I talked about the series of medical issues that led to his death. Before I knew it, we had been talking for hours, and it dawned on me that I was processing my feelings out loud, which felt very stabilizing and connective. You see, I had also been dealing with mental confusion, which I referred to as 'COVID brain'. I didn't want to speak too much about it or any subject for that matter. Me: the founder of a digital media and communications agency. I had been a spokesperson for top brand clients. My leadership impact depended on me to speak with authority and passion both internally and externally. I wasn't doing any of this. I was retreating inside for a long time, and I thought this fog, standstill, disconnection was the long-term effects of COVID-19, *long Covid* we're calling it now. Which from a branding perspective, sounds exactly as it should—ominous and awful! I also thought sometimes you just have to surrender to grief, but that didn't feel right to me either. I'm a fighter, a survivor born in New York City. *New York tough.* I was not going to surrender. It's a struggle that never leaves you, but you must find your own path to peace when you've lost big, bold love.

Then I listened to a discussion on the science of the brain at the precise time I couldn't concentrate or retain anything. I was in a daze, unable to focus, aimlessly mentally going in circles at times. My brain was focused on the feelings and symptoms of grief, not the tasks of the day. It was difficult to read and impossible to memorize. I had to do a series of podcasts with industry leaders during this time. I was terrible. It was very frightening, and I felt shame and hoped nobody would pick up on it. Listening to the interview on the brain, they said, "When you're going through grief and trauma, the emotion can become overwhelming and debilitating in numerous ways. It's sometimes referred to as 'grief brain' where your brain is being overloaded with thoughts of grief, sadness, loneliness, etc. It affects memory, concentration, and cognition. Your brain is focused on the feelings and symptoms of grief leaving little room for anything else. Your brain does not and cannot function properly. You're not able to find the right words naturally." *Wow*, I thought. What a relief! I was in denial of the effects of COVID-19 and the depression that comes with the severe grief of death making me feel mentally scattered and empty. This was very revealing. It rang true inside. It was a huge relief. I'm not losing my mind, I was grief stricken with sadness and it was affecting me cognitively, as well as emotionally, and might be a lingering effect of having had early COVID-19. I could use this information to carry me to next steps in my life review and ultimately, reinvention. If I understood the natural effects of grief, I didn't have to blame myself or feel shame every time I didn't quickly remember something critical or couldn't find the perfect word.

Negative self-talk doesn't serve anyone. Experts on death say the grief never completely ends, but the suffering is optional. Did you hear that? Suffering is optional. When someone dies, there's probate, the children, the bills. Jerry was also a visible partner in our company with pending projects and decisions that couldn't wait. I was trying to stay on top of all this, when on many nights, I wanted to pull the covers over my head and my dog, Willie's, and not give or respond to anything. Sometimes the fog is trying to slow you down so you can fully grieve. These abilities I prided myself on could return—and maybe in a stronger version—if I allowed myself to grieve properly, then review. Instead of burying me and my dog in the bed, which is devoid of meaning, I could switch my mindset to one of review and not put my entire well-being at risk with denial. Denial breeds isolation, anxiety, and unhealthy levels of stress. If COVID-19 didn't do the trick, severe stress makes you sick, showing up in at least twelve illnesses. That alone should jolt you into processing your feelings. If you're having a hard time being deliberate about reviewing what you're going through, or you're not in the space of sharing with others quite yet, write or audio-record it all out. No one is checking grammar, punctuation, or sequence of events. This is not the way we are designed to recall. Journaling your days of grief can be healing, but you must journal gratitude each day as well. I would also use voice memo on my phone to record when having an important client conversation that had to be remembered with precision.

What matters is that you know where you are at this moment. It's an intense personal journey. If you don't perform the review, you won't know you need reinvention. It's intervention! Before you know it, you will be able to relax and get a good night's sleep and look forward to promising mornings again. You will want to take care of yourself again. You will be in recovery and on your way to renewal.

I now live comfortably while also appreciating my husband's legacy. I use my married name of "Taylor" more often to connect and honor him. It gives me comfort.

SAMANTHA LUX AND IRENE BRANK: DIARY OF UNICORNS

Samantha Lux is a social media influencer and YouTube content creator who has amassed 630,000 subscribers and 60 million channel views. She uses her platform to promote social change, specifically aiming to reduce discrimination against the transgender community. I'm all ears but wait…there's more! For these Radical Reinvention tips, she's coming in an exciting package deal with her mother, Irene Brank, who leads a Learning & Performance Team and serves as her company's Pride ERG Vice Chair, Transgender Liaison & Gender Transition Partner.

Their reinvention as individuals, roles models, spokespeople, and as a family is nothing short of ultraradical.

Realization must lead to reinvention.

When I think of Radical Reinvention, this is a big switch living as a male to living as a girl. There was no other option. When I realized I was trans, it was like a truck hitting me. There was no way out of it. There was no way around it. I was going to have to deal with it. That was my path.

The moments mimicked the scene in "Little Miss Sunshine". The son realizes he can't fly a plane because he's colorblind. His whole world comes crashing down. I had this vision of my life and how I planned on things going, what steps to take, and who I was going to be in the future, then when I realized I needed to transition, it was like that "Little Miss Sunshine" moment when everything I had planned was no longer possible. I had always wanted to be on YouTube and talk about things via video to an audience, but I didn't think I could do it as a trans person. Who's going to want to watch a trans person on YouTube? It was an internal battle: This is who I am, who I want to be, what I have to do, but I still want to follow my dreams.

Identify your why, which will carry you through the pain.

The most exciting part was being able to let go of all these pressures and expectations of what everybody else had for me. Boys are supposed to act a certain way and do certain things. Those voices constantly telling me, "You're not going to be a cool boy. You're not a normal boy." Being able to let go of that was a big relief. When the surgeries finally came, it was part of the path. This was about my own alignment, my journey. Being able to be proud of who I am and work my dreams into it.

Truth is not conformation; truth is breath.

My dad and I didn't have the best relationship growing up because I was trying so hard to fit into his perception of what a boy was and I could never live up to it. It was heartbreaking for me. Now that I can let go and be myself, he sees me a lot happier, confident, and he's able to get to know me and understand the pressures I placed on myself. When I first transitioned, I would either try to hide it or try to make guys more comfortable with me being trans and deal with others' insecurities. Now, I go into it and say, "Just so you know, I'm trans and I hope that's okay and if it's not, that's okay too, I'm not here to convince you of anything. I am who I am and I'm not going back pre-reinvention."

Know you can't chase after your dreams if you don't reinvent. It might not be exactly what you had planned or the path you set out, but there are ways to make everything happen. If I had to transition again, I wouldn't think of my physical transformation first. I tried to conform to what society thinks a girl is. I would have tried to reframe my mindset, so I didn't think of it like that. It needed to solely be for me, my body, my image, my identity. Importantly, reality is not all beautiful right now. From society, there are so many attacks on trans people and mainly against trans youth. This is the hardest part in acting on reinvention. It's scary, but you need to do your best to live your truth.

Irene reinvented as Samantha's parent.

There's no greater reinvention than what Samantha has undergone. We also don't hear enough on how the family must reinvent upon gender transition. If 5 percent of the world is trans, and maybe more since you can still get killed depending on what country you live in, that means we're the cool parents that got one. But there's no role model for this. What am I supposed to be like? What am I supposed to do? How do I reinvent this world I live in? We socialize our children to be a certain sex. How do we keep her safe as a girl on campus? Help her reinvent herself in college? We teach girls never walk alone in a garage, always cover your drink at the bar, keep your keys out to stab someone in the eye.

Don't wait until it's too late to rebrand.

Reinvention comes from a reason. We don't just wake up and reinvent. When I talk to corporations, I tell them, you're going to have to reinvent. Don't wait until it's too late. Make sure you have policies and procedures for people to transition while they work for you. Don't be the company that just flies the Pride flag in June. People will look under the hood to see if you're supporting gender identity, pronouns, etc. If you wait, you will call me and say we need help today, which is always difficult. And you're not gonna hire the young people who are curious intellectuals, who you want. If you don't support the world they live in, they won't work for you.

My personal reason for reinventing myself was protecting my child. We never said, "If our kids are blond, then we'll keep them and be good parents!" I'm not even close to the same person. Neither is our family. First, I needed to realize my husband loves his kids *no matter what*. I worried because I was a different person then. Now I realize there was never any question of the person he is. Samantha even said, "He may hate what I am, but he loves me." Our other daughter was at the table, and someone said, "Why all this hoopla about the pronouns?" He said, "Because they're nonbinary!" This was not the same man I married.

I went to my physical the other day. My doctor said, "I heard you and Sam are speaking all over the country." How did you hear that? "Tom told me all about it!" I couldn't even imagine my husband starting that conversation.

Be your own unicorn.

As a mom, I got a unicorn, and not everyone gets one. Why did I get one? Why do I get the privilege of having a unicorn in my house? Maybe 70 million of us got one. I'm special. I get to have one of these very unique people in the world. And why doesn't everyone hire trans people? Sam is white. She has seen the world and the world has seen her as a white male. Now she lives as a woman and sees the world as a woman. The perspective transgender people have is 100 percent different than ours. They are the rarest asset you could possibly get with a perception very few people can have.

Reinvention is an individual thing.

It's important to honor what "transition" means for you. For everyone, it's different. I am working with a woman who says, "Below the waist doesn't bother me. I want breasts." For Samantha, it was everything. Is this type of reinvention a risk? Hell yes, in every sense of the word. It's not easy. It has to come from within. All motivation is intrinsic. Some people will shy away from that spark, the need to reinvent inside, or you can just go for it to be the better person, to be the next you. It's a choice. Everyone in this whole world will go through something that requires change, whether radical or not. If you've come out of a tragedy with life to still live, give that reinvention your best shot.

Reflection on Samantha Lux's Radical Reinvention

Imagine the steady supply of courage and confidence needed for Samantha's RADICAL REINVENTION. I know many people my age who resist basic levels of self-reflection, yet Samantha entered the realm of unbridled self-awareness, then she couldn't return to her former self. Couldn't think the same or look the same. She needed to carry on through the whole process of her transition to align with Samantha, no one else. I am so pleased she had her mother, Irene, by her side the whole way, who supported and protected her—while also overseeing the reinvention of her dad and the whole family. Their courage is contagious. I applaud them all. Such brave people tackling tough and uncomfortable work while self-protecting all the way through. Too bad it's not always like this. Let's hope together it gets better.

CHAPTER 2

RECOVER

"I believe that one defines oneself by reinvention. To not be like your parents. To not be like your friends. To be yourself. To cut yourself out of stone."

HENRY ROLLINS,
MUSICIAN

Stage 2 of Your Radical Reinvention—RECOVER
Resolution and Recommendations for:

Self-care | Sleep | Therapy | Sex | Nature | Exercise

I TOOK DAVID Kessler's advice: Find meaning in the moments. So much more rewarding than punching a pillow and scaring my dog in the process! Our first Thanksgiving was beautiful. I shopped for all the food and then together, me and my family cooked and baked with the music cranked up and our usual dancing with the dog while cooking in the kitchen. My son took over the grilling responsibilities from his dad and he's now a pro. It felt normal. It felt safe again.

I live in a state of gratitude and sadness. The two realities can co-exist. In fact, they must. There must be a happy ending in your life. Many happy endings. Be as gentle with yourself as you are with others. But you have to start to live bravely and have the courage to recover. One morning, I went outside and deeply experienced the flowers and heard the birds in a colorful sensory overload. I began to feel happy…then I wanted to tell Jerry. I worked hard in my mind to replace melancholy with joy, as much humor as possible and deep gratitude. This is the start of self-care.

Moments are memories. If you do not review your feelings and go to dark places if you must, you won't be present or mindful enough to make precious memories. I will always remember that morning I recognized again the delights of nature right outside my door. Nature and wellbeing are intertwined. Perhaps the earth's other living gems are not something we think about every day, but just as stress is linked to a great deal of illness and suffering, which we need to think more of, nature is of course, synonymous with clean air, clean water, nutritious food, and wellness, mentally and physically. That's not all.

Writing for *Forbes*, Tracy Brower says nature as a super elixir is trending. I thought nature was trending always. "New science finds key elements of nature which contribute most significantly to your happiness and wellbeing. A sweeping analysis recently published in *Science Advances* included 301 separate studies across 62 countries, wow!

The research identified many ways nature impacts people. It can contribute in meaningful ways to your cognition and the quality of your thinking. Get me outside! It can help you feel greater cohesiveness with the people around you, and even inspire better communication. It can also help you feel more creative, and it can help you develop—in terms of your character and confidence. There is also evidence nature can make you more reflective and give you a sense of renewal. And it can help you tap into your intuition and feel more inspired to move forward."

This summary alone speaks to several elements of Radical Reinvention: happiness, clear thinking, communication, creativity, confidence, renewal, inspiration. Yep, give me more sun, flowers, green grass, sand, oceans, and birds! Once I synchronized with them, even for a few minutes every day, the elements made deposits into my recovery bank. I could feel it in my body and the calmness that washed over me. This had a cumulative effect countering my sadness. To manage stress and anxiety, I also participated in 'grounding techniques' like walking barefoot in the grass or sand at the beach, and digging in the garden, which connected me to the earth's replenishing energy, enabling me to absorb electrons through direct bodily contact with the earth's surface to help revive and restore both body and mind. I felt awe, and I was reminded of being a part of a huge planet. Not insignificant but significant in my happiness and contributions as an individual among the significance of all life. I had to keep going in my recovery. Getting into nature and into the sun helped me significantly and it will help you too.

Brower's findings seem to concur: "Neuroscience

research highlighted in *The Happiness Hypothesis* finds experiences of awe and flow are associated with reduction in activity in the parts of the brain which are vigilant and self-focused. And studies by the University of California found awe-inspiring experiences caused the release of proteins called cytokines which had positive effects on happiness, wellbeing, and creativity. Feeling small in relationship to the vastness of nature provides perspective and appreciating the intricacies of a butterfly's wing can liberate you from a preoccupation with yourself. Focusing more on the bigger picture tends to predict positive experiences."

What access to nature do you have? Have you hugged a tree lately? This simple act is replenishing. Get outside. The beauty of nature besides the magical elements of nature itself is that it is infinite, coming in many forms. If you're not a birds-and-bees person, what about trees? Water, mountains, air, and most importantly, sun. Get outside and explore. And never underestimate the importance of stillness. This is all about self-nourishing. Besides its acclaim as the most filmed location in the world, Central Park in the center of New York City has been flagged as the "most visited urban park in the United States" with an estimated 50 million people every year. How many people visiting Central Park are going through Radical Reinvention? I suspect many. I'm one of them. What do you think?

Do You Want to Talk About It?

Everyone has given me names of therapists, triggering skepticism and the daunting task of weeding through matches as you would in the dating game. It's delicate.

Don't misunderstand me. I believe that the greatest gift we could give ourselves is the 'gift of therapy' to better understand our behavior, understand flaws and why the same mistakes are made. Some of the women I most admire have credited therapy to their emotional and professional success, so once, years ago, before another reinvention, I had a ninety-minute session with a therapist who triggered a real mind shift. My friend and business mentor, Jan, recommended her to me. She said, "I never would have been so successful and sold my company had it not been for therapy, which helped me in my hiring practices, see mistakes, analyze decisions." That therapist helped me, too, become more enlightened about myself, but she moved away within months. I only had a few sessions, but I felt the magic of talking about myself and being heard. You may be surprised to hear this, but I do not talk about myself, which makes writing a personal memoir an anomaly for me and many of my friends. Regrettably, I didn't continue therapy. I have an instinct to do it my way. Not always sound thinking on my part.

Inside my recovery period, I had traps that wouldn't let me take healthy walks. The traps may have spawned out of the grieving process because I had never experienced this before. Was I punishing myself in some way? I wondered. This is a natural default theory for not doing something that you know will improve your wellbeing. You must be ready to thrive. I guess I was not ready and could barely survive in those early months. It sounds like the nonsense of self-chatter invading my pages, but this was all true.

Taking care of yourself and your health gives you strength and confidence. If you feel fatigued or won't look in the mirror for a week, how will you feel toward others? You're retreating (and not the vacation kind), not reinventing. And comparing yourself to others is not productive either. *I don't drink a lot, I don't eat recklessly, but I haven't had a massage in over two years, and I love massage. My skin is so dry. I need to be buffed and scrubbed. I haven't gone for a long hike since Jerry passed. Why not? This is the mind chatter from one night sitting at dinner, observing some of my women colleagues and evaluating each one and how healthy they all looked—glowing. I'm also in the beauty business, so I can't help but associate self-care with health, appearance, and confidence.*

Happiness shows and glows in our faces. We wear confidence or discord and disarray. Eyes shine with excitement or dim from sadness. During the infamous quarantine from COVID-19 in 2020, how many of you talked about not washing, dying, or coiffing your hair? This was not only due to "laziness"—although for that time period, even if so, you're excused! Our bodies are our homes, leaving the light on for everything we experience, good and bad. Ask yourself, is it time for more good? Your body will tell you. Mine is telling me at the very least to walk more, buff, scrub and get a massage. Self-care is not just about spa treatments that few can afford. The 6 life essentials are restorative sleep, nutrients and hydration, movement, sunlight and social connection.

Recovery is very individual. I need to be with family and friends as much as possible. I need to stay busy and keep moving. I need to be out with friends. My great friends, Jane and Steve, invite me to their home for dinner at least three times a week since Jerry passed. Their kindness and compassion are filled with pure love and goodness. I love when I know I'm going to see them for dinner and a movie. We call ourselves The Three Musketeers. It's such an important lifeline. I also need to keep working and feeling connected. That's my therapy. That's my salvation. What do you need for restoration after excavation and review? Music, movies and podcasts top my list, but only after I get that massage my body is yearning for. It could range from more connection with family and friends, yes, a spa weekend, a new mattress for better sleep, even "a new vibrator", as Dr. Ann Turner will tell you.

Okay, let's pause here for a moment. Are you getting good, restorative sleep? I mean deep and long sleep. It's worth stressing that without sleep, there is no reinvention. If you're not sure how good your sleep is, get an Oura ring. It's wearable tech that will tell you so much about your body, cramming all these sensors into one small ring. It tells you how your body is functioning and what it needs for optimum health. It's a sleep tracker and so much more. Check it out. Not expensive, but important.

Let's proceed.

For more than twenty years, Ann Turner's mission has been to help people develop their own personal 'resilience toolkits,' so they have the skills to cope with life's stressors—and reinvent anytime, like she has. Her Radical Reinvention was divorce, becoming a single mother, and remarrying. What are we talking about here? Relocation of her home and counseling practice, navigating the dating pool, blending families, and expanding her practice to incorporate sex therapy (there was evidence of an increased need for this post-COVID). She couldn't be happier, and of course, her life lessons are education for her clients, so she is sharing and giving back, emphasizing what all our Radical Re-Inventors have in common.

When I spoke with Dr. Turner, I was still struggling with my own loss and didn't want to talk about Jerry's death. Because of COVID-19, many people didn't even know that he'd died and there wasn't the typical ritual of a funeral right after his death that would announce it to the public; only a heartfelt tribute in the *New York Times* and a peaceful and celebratory dinner on his birthday for the children and a few friends. Dr. Turner suggested that instead of waiting and worrying others would bring it up at inopportune times or that they refuse to talk about Jerry for fear of making me sad, I needed to mention his death to acquaintances to get it out in the open and allow myself to talk about it on my terms and in my own way. Dr. Turner said this would allow me to be in charge of the narrative instead of passively reacting to the change process. I listened, but very infrequently brought up my husband's death. Didn't want to bring people down. She took her own advice and took charge of her own reinvention.

Dr. Turner has been divorced for eight years (separated for six years before that). Although divorce was devastating for her and her family, she used her knowledge about human behavior, resilience, happiness, and habit formation to get through this difficult time before working on her book, *Happy Divorce* (still in progress). "My happiness formula includes help, appreciation, passion, people, independence, nature, exercise, sleep, sex. I'm learning more in my sex therapy training and getting specialized training. When I was single for many years, I missed holding someone's hand. Little things." I continue to be curious about this special training.

I know what Dr. Turner means by the little gestures of intimacy. One night, my dog hopped into bed with me, and I could feel his breathing on my chest (and I can feel your anxiety from that opening sentence). I have missed that closeness, the beat of a heart. But there are always gains that inspire our reinvention if we are still breathing. That's always a good start, Dr. Turner insists. "It's exciting. The beauty of our world right now is you can be who you want to be. I can put something online and reinvent how people see me and get immediate validation."

Pain drives persistence if you're on the right track—meaning, you have reviewed the raw materials of your circumstances. Dr. Turner did. "I had to let go of my old life—my address, my neighbors, two kids in elementary school. It was realizing that I can change myself and that I don't need to focus on, nor should I try to change, my ex. What happens with divorce is you get in a mindset of demonizing your spouse as opposed to saying, 'Who cares what they are doing? I have me and I have to move forward. And I have children. What is my next chapter? I can't control the other person's crazy stuff. When my marriage started having weird things happen like mysterious charges on my credit card bill, I started to write it down because I thought I was losing my mind or maybe overreacting. I wanted my girls to know that there were cracks that were starting to show in our marriage and how much I struggled with the very big and consequential decision to get a divorce. 'He said he would meet us at the shore, and he didn't show up.' Things were increasingly wrong.

If I ever got a divorce, I wanted to be able to justify why I broke up with their dad. I didn't want my girls to see me as dependent, weak. I had to show them Mom's gonna be okay so they can be okay. I grew up far away from my own dad, who lived in Tennessee while I lived with my mom in Rhode Island. Then I had this awful situation in my marriage; he wanted joint custody. This is a guy who didn't come home for dinner during the week! But when we separated, he finally did it. He stepped up. We lived a few blocks from each other, which was good for the girls. I was divorced for many years and dated so many people. So much radical shit happened! On a date, this guy showed me the picture of another woman, who he just had sex with." What a douche.

It's clear that children help you navigate the "radical shit" Dr. Turner speaks of. I didn't want my son, Nick, to feel my pain, in addition to his own profound grief, but he was there with me every step of the way. He was there for his father, for me, for the family. Dedicated. Courageous. When Jerry was severely ill, Nick had been there to help his father with everything he needed including to inject his blood thinners into his stomach every night. He became my 'care partner' in trying to get Jerry well with inventive meals and shakes, walking together to get his mobility back, pool workouts, slow dancing together at dinner and just filling his life with love, peace, joy, and lots of laughter. Because COVID-19 was raging, my husband's other two wonderful children, Scott and Julie, lived in other states and it was profoundly sad that they couldn't visit with their dad as often as they would have liked. Just another horror of the virus and its isolation.

When we lost Jerry, Nick motivated me to get up, get dressed and put the face on. At the very least, act alive, even when I didn't feel that zest in my cells. This was the same son, who, for my birthday, gave me a beautifully crafted bamboo bowl full of 365 handwritten notes with photos on why he loved me. What a bright light, what a reason to get up every morning feeling whole! Besides my work, Nick reminded me there is life after such profound loss...and a chance for another happy reinvention. My son also gave me the gift of a marriage to his sweetheart of over five years, Holly. She lived with us during COVID and my husband adored her, and she adored him, and that's very important. Who am I now? I'm not a wife or a married woman. What I am is a damn good mother and that brings meaning, pride, joy, love and allows me to look forward to the future and what it might bring. The memories and my beautiful son bring me back into the light.

Everyone is searching for happiness. People need a formula more than ever. Dr. Turner adds: "Appreciate your life. These tips for happiness are accessible to all people. No. 4 in the happiness formula is *people*. One client has toxic sisters and mom. So many people get stuck in toxic relationships. They don't break free, and it affects other aspects of their lives. It slows their growth, their reinvention certainly. This may be due to low self-esteem. You can change your self-esteem. You can boost it. Especially during an event like separation and divorce. Use the time, use the pain and uncertainty. The opposite is secure attachments, and you can learn how to form more of these especially if you do step No. 1, which is to get help and look at why you form non-secure attachments."

Start with these steps and start feeling happier and better. Start feeling hopeful.

- **H**ELP: Enlist in therapy, professional support.
- **A**PPRECIATION: Express gratitude.
- **P**ASSION: Find your passion/career/volunteer.
- **P**EOPLE: Spend the "right" amount of time with people who aren't toxic.
- **I**NDEPENDENCE: Gain financial and mental independence for yourself.
- **N**ATURE: Get out in nature.
- **E**XERCISE: Get moving.
- **S**LEEP: Optimize your wake/sleep cycles.
- **S**EX: Get your physical needs met.

A period of restoration will help you reinvent because you can think more clearly. At this stage, you feel and reflect, but you don't stay stuck in ruminating. Here, you'll get past your denial of the events that transpired and rocked your world into needing to reinvent. Use your experience to appreciate how far you've come and reimagine what you want to do next. "Bravely living and ready to recover" was my mantra.

LIZ G. BAILEY: NOT ANOTHER NIGHT

Liz G. Bailey is a survivor, mother, published author, speech-language pathologist, and podcast host. With a master's degree in communication sciences and as a survivor of domestic violence, she knows what it means to use your voice to protect yourself and the ones you love. Bailey began freelance writing for online publications focusing on parenting, relationships, spiritual growth, and self-help. After bravely leaving an abusive marriage, she continued her healing journey by attending domestic violence groups and advocating for women and families in her hometown of Austin, Texas. When she is not writing or teaching others how to use their voices, she is busy networking, interviewing, and editing for her podcast, "The Pretty Truth". Here, she tells us her pretty truth and gives sound advice for leaving an abusive relationship and making yourself radically happy through reinvention.

Determine what need is being met by staying and if your actions are rational.

Radical means "a lot". "Unexpected". Even though it's hard. I landed in a second marriage, and it was full of overt and covert types of abuse, many of which I didn't understand because I had no framework for it. I didn't grow up with abusive men, nor did I marry one the first time around. My fear of being poor and the mindset I developed from childhood led me to a man who made good money, promising me security and fancy things. That was the sort of love bombing I experienced, and it worked. It wasn't that he was playing to my ego. He was playing to my fears, the vulnerabilities I told him in confidence and perceived safety. Eventually I realized the physical rages, manipulation, and sexual coercion were abuse. I didn't know I was going through all of that until I started losing my sense of self. I have children and I didn't want them to see me like that or feel like similar relationships are okay. When I decided to leave, it was scary because not only was it the most dangerous time in an abusive relationship; I was also afraid of my financial safety rugs being pulled out from under me. I felt like I had to choose financial security over physical and emotional safety. How would I recover from this?

The reinvention started when I realized these two things are not mutually exclusive. I worked full time our entire marriage. It wasn't like I was sitting in a mansion eating bonbons and going to garden club events. I was working and mothering and helping to run a short-term rental business, all the while walking on eggshells to keep peace in the home and in the bedroom. I realized that I could, in fact, take myself out of the situation of timing conversations, worrying about which version or mood I would get, and finding ways to lie to my friends about what was really going on. The reinvention came when I believed I could be free in all the ways I deserved and desired.

Your intuition signals danger and more threats to come.

I could trace one of the red flags to early in the relationship, thinking, *I don't want to make him angry.* I didn't pinpoint why. Then in the first physical altercation, I did make him angry, and I paid for it. After one of the last physical assaults when I thought I was going to die, I truly started to fade away. The fear and trauma from that moment and that night left me blank and empty, floating through days, trying not to feel scared all the time. He later told me, "If I wanted you dead, I would have killed you. I was just trying to scare you." He had my life in his hands and chose not to take it. He was blackout drunk, but when people came to help, he was cool as a cucumber. It was all about coercion, control, and fear tactics. I knew I was not meant to live like that.

Beware of patterns that suck up your energy.

The hardest part of my reinvention was taking old storylines and programs that led me to the relationship (and some that were formed during the trauma and fear of the relationship) and having to swim against those tides. I had to remember that my thoughts create my reality and that I was more capable than I was given credit for. I was not going to be on the streets if I filed for divorce. I am educated and employed. I was not incapable of commitment. I stayed loving and loyal for way too long. And I certainly did not end my marriage because I don't care about my family. Family is what you make it. And I want mine to live a safe and happy existence. I want my children to experience what healthy relationships look and feel like, so they have a chance at making good choices with and for their partners. You have to reinvent from the inside out! I dispelled old stories and I won!

I love social media, but you see so many things that are all toxic positivity. Some of it is quite lovely with words and images that resonate with me, but until I start to live and embody some of those reinvented thought patterns, a beautifully written meme on Instagram doesn't do much. I have to practice because I know that a series of thoughts will turn into a belief, and a belief will turn into action. So, when I tell myself I am good enough, I believe that and more. I am worthy of respect and attention. I am allowed to feel a full spectrum of emotion without being called "too much" or "too sensitive." I'm not bad at relationships or at "picking people." The valuable lessons from this are innumerable. As I change those thought patterns, I believe more and more in myself, which is a radical internal reinvention.

There are still times where something feels scary financially or I wished I had a partner. I'm sad sometimes when I'm doing certain things alone, like making calls about the mortgage or going on group vacations. Those, along with many other scenarios far less glamorous, can be scary enough to make you stay. You'll tell yourself things like "He's got more income than I do," "At least I'm not alone," or "I don't want to look bad in front of my friends," to name a few.

So many of these social expectations got slapped on us and we just stick to them, often placing our own dreams and our own happiness on the shelf. One thing I have realized is that whether I am doing what everyone else is doing is not the key to my peace. The focus is inside of me and comparing my journey to everyone else's was one of the most harmful things I could do to my self-worth and trust.

Abuse has clear signs.

I learned in therapy that when you are in an abusive relationship, you find yourself confused and that is very much by design. You are meant to be turned upside down because if you don't know which way is up, you're more likely to stay put because it feels at the least disorienting. You will begin to question your own reality because it's being questioned and convoluted by the person who is supposed to love and support you. However, you define your relationship, when your body and your brain are telling you something feels wrong, it's important to listen. Your gut, your intuition knows. So, get curious with yourself. Ask yourself questions like: Am I tired or overreacting? Am I reacting or responding? Am I allowed to have a grievance or is everything being blamed on me? Notice if you are having a discourse or being shut down.

There are overt and covert types of abuse and the

misinformation about what is and isn't considered "real" domestic violence, and who is considered a "real" victim is intensely harmful. If your experience doesn't involve bruises or broken bones, then your cries are often ignored. When someone is breaking your things, stalking you, calling you names, beating you down emotionally until you don't know who you are anymore, you are being abused and it should be addressed.

Self-assurance has no comparison.

I was riddled with self-doubt and thought I needed to stay. Then I was afraid for my life and knew I had to leave. I took that fear and put it into action. I learned and planned my way out—and got out. I took my past programming and my current situation and turned it into something new. I knew I could do it. I went from wondering how I would support my family, trust myself, and feel whole to affirming my worth and bolstering my belief that my intuition knew all along. A pivotal moment came when I (secretly) read the book, *Why Does He Do That*, by Lundy Bancroft. Someone finally put words to my experiences and validation to my fears. For the first time, I was able to envision a different future. So, I started putting money away. I opened a separate bank account, told only my mom, and urged her not to ask questions. I just needed support. I started taking little steps to chip away at my fear of leaving. Then COVID-19 hit. I was stuck. And the bad behavior on his part didn't stop. It pushed me to do more to get out. Before the pandemic, we trialed a separation, which did not go well. Then with the world on lockdown, we felt like we "needed" each other. He didn't want to be alone, and I wasn't able to work. As the world was trying to figure itself, and I was slowly fading into a shadow of myself, I hit a tipping point. And my desire to leave him finally outweighed my fear of leaving him.

In whatever you are reinventing, ask yourself if you are doing good. For yourself, for your community, and the world at large? Your reinvention is for your higher self. I didn't know that I wanted to write a book, be an advocate, speak, and completely change the course of my life until I endured, reflected, resolved to act, and 'took my power back.' Domestic violence is pervasive. This is happening to a lot of people. How could I help? How could I use what I went through to be of service to others? How could I grow and shine and show up for myself and my loved ones from a courageous and humbled place? Searching for those answers, for purpose from pain, was my driving force to reinvent.

Reflection on Liz's Radical Reinvention

Liz reclaimed her power and independence after literally being beaten into submission to someone else's life narrative for her. She was in a great deal of danger, and it would take twice as much bravery to pull not only herself but also, two little ones from a volatile home life—and overcome her deep-rooted fear of financial insecurity. She built herself up again to write amazing new chapters of being a role model and helping others see that leaving an abuser and reinventing is possible. If you take away one lesson from this book, believe me when I stress the need for women to be financially and emotionally independent. It is so critical. Additionally, I must stress the importance of your own separate bank account and having money that's yours alone to protect yourself and your family.

CHAPTER 3

REAWAKEN

"If you are curious, you'll find the puzzles around you. If you are determined, you will solve them."

—*Erno Rubik, inventor*

Stage 3 of Your Radical Reinvention—REAWAKEN

Resolution and Recommendations for:

Imagination | Enchantment | Creativity
| Inquiry | Knowledge | Discovery

Are you awake now? You've accomplished the first big, scary phases of Radical Reinvention, and things will begin to feel intriguing. You don't want to miss out on the sensations of reawakening—your imagination and creativity. In fact, cleansing your palette of grief, depression, fright, and uncertainty moves you into an active loop of discovery, which can make you feel more alive than ever. Discovery becomes irresistible as it morphs into knowledge. It stirs exhilaration and enchantment. There is no comparison to these feelings as the soil for growth.

I was raised on the Upper West Side of New York City. I thought of myself as a strong, confident, and somewhat tough, young girl living with and competing with two brothers. I very much related to "Scout" in Harper Lee's book, *To Kill a Mockingbird*, with overalls, never dresses, pigtails and bangs, bruised knees and following my big brother, Billy. And I idolized my father, like Scout. He was my hero. I could roller-skate fast and furiously like a crazy person holding on to New York City buses to get there faster. I played stick ball and stoop ball with all my brothers' friends. I liked to wrestle—with the boys only. Once, on a dare, I put my head between two railings on our city block and it got stuck. My mother had to call the fire department to free me. Daring, but maybe not always so smart.

I was free and invincible, so I thought. Suddenly, gangs started appearing in this very family-friendly part of the city and they would come up behind me and try to pull me into Riverside Park. I lived at 108th and Riverside Drive. It would begin to get dark, and I would have to fight back to avoid them crowding around purposely trying to scare me and get me to go to the park with them. It was terrifying, but I'd fight back.Around this same time, there was a man waiting outside of my school and he would follow me home every day. If I went to the Five and Dime, he would be there. He seemed to be everywhere I was after school. This man really frightened me. My instinct of possible harm was ever present even as a young girl. I was only ten or eleven years old. All these years later, I can still see his sinister face in my mind. One night, I broke down to my parents about my stalker and the personal fear of these new gangs and what was happening to me very often in the city. I knew I was in danger and couldn't live with it any longer. Within months, we moved out of New York City to Leonia, New Jersey where my grandmother, aunts and cousins lived and eventually Short Hills, New Jersey. It would be a period of discovery.

I entered Millburn High School as a junior. It's hard to come into a new school in your junior year and make new friends. I think of that time as an early reinvention for me. All relationships start in kindergarten or that vital school age. Reinvention skills are activated early. It's like our own school preparing us for bigger reinventions later in our life.

In my junior year of high school, the challenges and environments were drastically different from all that I knew. Millburn is one of the best schools in the country. I came from a Catholic school, and it was night and day. My new school was more scholarly, and I learned the beauty of learning and education there. I became a voracious reader and an excellent student by comparison to the previous school. Mr. Ross, my English teacher and early mentor, gave me the curiosity, exploration and joy of reading and learning. It was thrilling. I had renewed confidence. My life was dramatically changed moving to this school in this town at this time in my life.

As a teen, how was I going to get through this? At this age *then*, you didn't look at your life in terms of pivoting and jumping off the deep end. *Now*, you prepare your kids for everything. In those days, it was go to school and talk about it, or not, that night. In the junior year, friendships have been developing for years; it was hard to break in and be accepted. However, I remember employing a lot of creative thinking on the school bus, including what I was wearing down to the hair, a little makeup, a circle pin, and saddle shoes. I remember assessing the situation. Where is all the power? *Oh, I see who has it. That girl over there checking me out. She's really popular, I need to get closer to her.* I imagined beguiling her with humor. I conceived a strategy even at the age of sixteen.

The next day, I embarked on my goal of captivating her and making her laugh, which was easy for me. It worked. Then her friends started moving in. I had imagined what would appeal to this girl and acted out scenarios in my very active mind. I also knew that if I didn't have inroads into a friendship circle, I wouldn't have social capital for the next two years of high school. Academic achievement is hard enough at this age, but the need to belong is largely affirmation or death to identity even at that young age. In my mission, I had me and my imagination, not a lot of life experience, but my plan worked. What was I doing? I was reinventing myself to just fit in and have friends. I was building my personal brand. I didn't know it at the time, but it's clear to me now.

Fellow PR tribesman and "idea whisperer" Mitch Markson wrote and drew and photographed the book, *The Imagination Playbook,* a guide to help you be more imaginative, playful, and purposeful with your brand, whether that brand is you, your product/service, your organization, or an identifying issue you are passionate about. Inside, you learn how to feel more comfortable with the designations of Imagination and Creativity and find and flex your imagination and creativity muscles with "playtime" activities, imagination-stirring tools, not rules, a personal branding guide, and a social issue-to-brand primer with plenty of examples. To trigger your ideas, he recommends listing five to ten things that stimulate your imagination, such as dreams and nightmares, graffiti or street art, movies, and five to ten idealists who inspire you, such as inventive writer and filmmaker, Guillermo Del Toro. Who inspires you?

I, for one, am thrilled that Mitch wrote this innovative book as a testament to the power of using a major asset we all start to develop before the age of two! Albert Einstein said, "Logic will get you from A to B. Imagination will take you everywhere."

One venue that has always made my imagination pop is movies. My son and I share this love and are constantly talking about and watching all the new movies that stream and screen. As a teenager with my brothers watching James Bond movies, I was mesmerized, and my imagination ran wild. This was a world new to me. Not by James leaping and tumbling into his next adventure, but by the 'Bond Girls.' I didn't know women could have this kind of life. I thought, *I want to be a Bond Girl! I want to travel to exotic places. I want to be powerful. I want to be smart. I want respect from men, I want to be fierce, mentally and physically. And of course, I want beautiful clothes. Most importantly, I want independence, financially and emotionally. I will give myself that, I will work hard and find it no matter what. These images from the Bond movies gave me an early ambi-*

tion oriented toward power, life success, financial security, travel, and it has never left me to this day.

When I finished college, the place I wanted to work was *Vogue* or *Time* magazine. I don't think I had a deep conversation with my parents about what I wanted to do. But my mind was clear and determined at the age of twenty. I was free to imagine my future. I didn't know anyone who could help me even though my mom was in the fashion business. I didn't have anyone important calling for me or writing a letter. I didn't have social capital, which is easier to build up today due to all the connectivity tech we have. Connections are accepted with a click. Relationships must be nurtured just the same as they did then, but digital tools have rebranded the way we win professional opportunities.

I started my career with failure. All *Vogue* asked me to do as a prerequisite for getting in the door was to take a typing test, and I failed. I did not panic or cave. I jumped up and shouted, "I will be back!"

Secretarial school meant going into the city every day for six months from Short Hills. At this time, New York had it all and it was my city. I learned how to type ferociously, and when I came back, they couldn't believe I had the tenacity to go to typing school for six months to get a job at *Vogue*. Six of the most important months of my life. I turned that failure into a success of typing ninety words or more a minute. I became a typing fool in order to work for *Vogue* and it took just six months. Six months that radically changed my life. It was worth it and let me tell you why.

The most powerful woman in this world at this

moment was Mary Campbell, the head of HR and on the board of Condé Nast. She happened to be the person who interviewed me and ultimately hired me. What were the chances of her, the big boss, doing my interview? That was a lucky duck moment. How could she say no? Mary saw that I had passion and the fearlessness to return to try again. She was an Irish Catholic and I was an Irish Catholic and went to Marymount College in Virginia, and this shamelessly worked in my favor. This only occurred to me a few months ago when I was reviewing my career and how it all happened. Find people like you in power. We like and trust our own tribe. It works. They hired me on the spot as a rover (an "intern" in today's workplace).

Failure was transformational for me. It gave me the biggest career opportunity of my life. I got to know all the top magazine editors and interned for Si Newhouse, the owner of Condé Nast, for three months, as well as Alex Liberman, the renowned editorial director, for several months. The contacts I made in that first year interning at Condé Nast have served me well to this day and helped lead me ultimately to the powerful 'Bond Girl' life I so desired, but on my terms.

As a twenty-year-old walking into that building, I remember the sensations I felt like it was yesterday. I went to the ladies' room and saw editors I knew from studying the magazines. I was always pinching myself. You cannot put a price on passion, imagination, and enchantment. After almost a year of interning at all the big magazines published by Condé Nast, I got the position I wanted in the fashion department of *Vogue*. You certainly cannot put a price on my first trip to Paris alongside the legendary editor-in-chief, Diana Vreeland. I was captivated by her vibrancy and unique language of fashion, beauty, and creative innovation. I had never met anyone like Mrs. Vreeland then or since. She was always daringly different and somewhat frightening, and she became an inspirational mentor for life. She departed just about eighteen months after I arrived.

Working at *Vogue* in those days was a total reinvention. You had to look the part, which meant you couldn't eat. Right, you could not eat! You had to speak the part and honor certain fashion cues like they were sacred prayers. I remember my father bought me a weekender Vuitton bag, and that was a cue that I didn't realize at the time. I was *Vogue* material amongst all these socialites, people of money and people who had been at the magazine a long time, but I didn't even realize it at the time. I was always the youngest person. I was in at 8:30 just to send the right message I was serious, and I always stayed late usually packing trunks for shoots going to exotic lands with the top models and photographers of the day. It was exciting every single day. Celebrities would come every day to visit with Mrs. Vreeland. Celebrities like the Beatles, the Stones, the Prince of Wales, Twiggy, Jean Shrimpton, and Lauren Hutton virtually lived at *Vogue*. They were all there so they could be in *Vogue*. Just like me.

Amazingly, I lived on the same street, on East 73rd, as Samuel (Si) Newhouse. It was hard to get cabs there. I would see him, and we often shared cabs. It was serendipitous. I always had the cash to pay for both of us since he "always only had a hundred-dollar bill" as he would tell me when the cab stopped. You just cannot make this shit up.

Again, I was an intern at the time; translation: no extra cab money laying around! At the time, I didn't know his role at the magazine. Then Mr. Newhouse asked HR for me personally to step in when his assistant took a medical leave of absence for several months. When I arrived at his office that morning, I was shocked. I had thought he worked in the art department with a few other icons. I didn't know he was the CEO/owner of Condé Nast! I guess I had made a positive impression during our short but financed-by-me cab rides. As my mother would often say, "You never know your luck in a big town."

A few years later, I worked for an editor much older who I didn't feel would take me any further, so I was going to leave the magazine to work for a famous interior designer. Time to reimagine. I confidentially informed a woman at *Vogue* in a senior position, and she went to Si telling him that they were about to lose someone they should keep. He quipped, "We'll give Maureen that job!" My enthusiasm, knowledge of the business, work ethic and training had given me the confidence to make a move when I was feeling unsure. At that time, I became the youngest woman on the *Vogue* masthead. Yeah me.

FERN MALLIS: REINVENTING THE FASHION INDUSTRY

Fern Mallis grew up in a family that worked in the Garment District, with her father excelling as a super salesman of women's scarves. From very early on, she loved clothing. In high school in Brooklyn, Fern was voted "Best Dressed". That was the beginning, and she knew she would do something in the fashion industry. That "something" blossomed into instrumental positions that transformed the industry worldwide, placing American designers on the same world map as European designers with the formation of New York Fashion Week. Fern is always described by and introduced with "another reinvention".

Here, Fern tells all that went into imagining and devising a risky Radical Reinvention involving numerous sectors, stakeholders, livelihoods, and the face of fashion forever.

Develop skills and relationships simultaneously.

I attended University of Buffalo and while there, joined *Mademoiselle* magazine's College Board. At that time, so many writers and leading editors came out of *Mademoiselle*. It was the pinnacle of fashion/beauty publications. In 1969, when I was selected as one of twenty guest editors in this prestigious competition, I followed in the footsteps of previous guest editors such as Joan Didion, Betsey Johnson, Sylvia Plath. I embarked on a month of focus groups, interviewing people, industry parties, and a trip to Israel. I got to shadow a senior editor and it was a remarkable experience. At *Mademoiselle*, I noticed no one had colored nails. You have to look and observe and adjust your own personal style. The new clear nails helped.

After the month-long guest editorship, *Mademoiselle* offered me a fulltime job. I started my career by winning a contest!

I moved into merchandising and marketing, organizing fashion events and shows in every major department store all over the country. I did this for several years, and then came my first reinvention: leaving the magazine and working at a wholesale fashion company, but this was one stop in the road. Then I became a fashion director at Gimbels East responsible for windows, special events and trend forecasting. Here, my career blossomed.

I was always helping friends out with events and resources and contacts to make their events more memorable. This led to me starting my own PR agency and working with fashion and interior furnishings clients on their events. One of my first assistants was Jane Hertzmark (now Hudis), and she's become Global Group President of The Estee Lauder Companies. Proudly for me, she's one of the most impressive and important executives in the cosmetics industry. She spent her first six years working for me, and she's considered family.

Both your skills and relationships serve you for a lifetime of reinventions.

Join disciplines and skill sets in your climb (sometimes there are no clear titles).

To me, *everything* is PR! I became a specialist in product launches, parties, and press kits. We sprinkled glitter and confetti in envelopes. All our materials and invites stood out on your desk. We wanted our clients to be noticed. All my disciplines intertwined. I could never understand how people could dress well and not live in a beautiful environment or eat beautifully presented food? It's all a connected taste level.

As my firm expanded, one of my clients was the IDCNY (International Design Center NY), who I later worked fulltime for as senior VP of marketing and advertising. I spent several years celebrating designers and architects in the interior furnishings industry. There were many mindboggling, showstopping projects.

In 1990, there was a massive recession and the real estate boom stopped. Everyone stopped buying furniture and constructing new buildings. IDCNY let me go, and I took a freelance job with a hot PR firm and brought my legendary triple Rolodex with me! I worked on a special project, "Color Day" with Pantone at the Cooper Hewitt

Design Museum. It was all about color in everything—advertising, fashion, food. We dyed all the cocktail foods different colors and people were freaking out by these gorgeous platters of blue, red, and purple food.

Stand out in whatever you do. It's the key to getting noticed and remembered. Don't compromise the details. Someone is always paying attention to the finishing touches.

Invest in industry events and amass contacts.

Back in the early 80s, I became a founding board member of DIFFA (Design Industry Foundation Fighting AIDS). We were doing a lot of fabulous events to raise money and awareness. We gave our first grant to Ganga Stone to buy an industrial/restaurant refrigerator for her startup organization, God's Love We Deliver. I did a delicious event called "Edible Architecture" with specialty bakers and designers using their creativity long before cooking and cupcake shows on cable TV. We auctioned off all these creations at Sotheby's, which raised $500,000, a ton of money at that time, I would do everything I could to raise money for so many of my pals who were dying of AIDS.

In the fall of 1990, Seventh on Sale became the fashion industry premier event produced by the Council of Fashion Designers of America (CFDA). I attended the dessert party, which was all I could afford. Anna Wintour, Donna Karan, Calvin Klein, and Ralph Lauren were the cochairs. This four-day shopping event was designed by Robert Isabel who had the best taste level and created the most extraordinary events and parties. Tickets to shop for two-hour sessions were $20, and there were lines around the block. All the designers were in their individually decorated spaces selling their clothes and accessories well below wholesale prices. It was amazing, as $5 million was raised.

After this successful event, the CFDA began a search for a new executive director. I threw my hat in the ring thanks to my friend, Jeffrey Banks, and others, who said I'd be perfect for that job. I found out that the CFDA had received hundreds of resumes. I sent mine in on a Friday and got called to come in for a meeting Monday. It was time to leverage my network. I had the first interview with Stan Herman and reminded him that I had interviewed him when I was a *Mademoiselle* guest editor. Next interview was with Calvin Klein, Bill Blass and CFDA President Carolyne Roehm. I knew Calvin from Fire Island days, and Bill Blass looked a bit like my dad. He said, "You've not been in fashion for ten years. Why should we hire you?" I said, "I never stopped wearing clothes, reading fashion magazines, shopping and staying up with the trends." They were also looking for someone who had experience raising funds for AIDS on the heels of their successful Seventh on Sale benefit.

Research and represent—even on your birthday.

For the final confirmation for this position, I was as nervous as a nellie because every designer on the CFDA board—a literal fashion who's who—were there.

I dressed for the part. I felt confident from what I had accomplished and saw the potential for this new position.

Still, it was a challenging meeting with lots of questions and back-and-forth discussions.

After a short while, I was asked to wait in an office while this group of famous designers deliberated. When I came back in the room, the entire board sang "Happy Birthday" to me and brought out a cake. It was a birthday I'll never forget, as the memories are burned in my brain. Sorry, there was no video or cell phones back then.

Get in the door and be perceptive about what problems to solve.

During the next two weeks before I started the job, it was Market Week. If there were fifty fashion shows, they were held in fifty different locations. The schedule would drive you insane because no one could possibly get to all these locations. No one talked to each other. No accountability. If you did something in the afternoon at The Plaza or The Pierre Hotel, there could be a wedding or bar mitzvah taking place later in the evening and next day, you'd have to pay for everything all over again.

In 1991, Michael Kors produced a show in an empty warehouse space in Chelsea. If you've ever been at a fashion show, you know when you turn up the bass music, if things aren't nailed down, they tend to shake and move. Well, the ceiling shook and moved. Chunks of plaster came down on the runway, onto the shoulders of the supermodels, because Michael only hired the best! Plaster chunks also landed in Carrie Donovan's lap, the fashion editor of *The New York Times*, along with Suzy Menkes from the *Inter-*

national Herald Tribune. They wrote the next day, "We live for fashion, we don't want to die for it."

I thought, *my job description just changed*. The industry had to do better. The industry had to Radically Reinvent.

I soon began to search New York City for an enormous empty space. I looked at every pier, parking lot, buildings that had stopped construction mid-stream because of the recession. We settled in what is now the Millennium Hotel and experimented for a few seasons to see if multiple designers would show in the same space. We made a deal with Bryant Park to set up several tents. I spent countless hours with a few assistants and a freelance producer who worked out of a closet in my office to coordinate this massive event. I spent weeks 'dialing for dollars' to raise the funds to implement this fashion village.

The centralized location would allow for everyone to come to the same address, hobnob with media covering the event, and eat in the same place. We had terrific sponsors providing services and amenities for the designers and the guests attending the shows. Our office had a 'war room' to organize the calendar and figure out who would be in what tent and at what time. This initiative put American designers on the map and launched many careers. Each season we would hire a new designer to illustrate the fronts. I loved these creative endeavors. Entering the tents at Bryant Park was a very heady experience. It was like fashion's equivalent of getting into Studio 54.

The last show produced at Bryant Park featured Tommy Hilfiger who thanked and acknowledged me and Stan Herman for all we did at Bryant Park for the fashion community for almost twenty years.

Reinventions run their course—know when to walk away or lose it all.

When I left CFDA to join IMG, I became global ambassador for Fashion Weeks and helped create and organize Fashion Weeks all over the world.

Leave a legacy.

After leaving IMG when the tents moved to Lincoln Center, it was my time to leave as well. I enjoyed taking time off to 'smell the roses' and relax. Then 92Y offered me a rare opportunity to interview designers. Fashion Icons with Fern Mallis was born, and my first one-on-one interview was with designer, Norma Kamali, then came Calvin Klein, Tom Ford, Marc Jacobs, Vera Wang, Betsey Johnson, Bill Cunningham, Michael Kors and many more. The first nineteen interviews became a book published by Rizzoli in 2015. A second book, *Fashion Icons 2*, featuring conversations with Valentino, Victoria Beckham, Zandra Rhodes, Tim Gunn, Leonard Lauder, Bob Mackie, Billy Porter, Iris Apfel, and many more was released in April 2022 with a huge launch party at Nordstrom, who sponsored the book.

These designers had never been interviewed in this way. They talked about being bullied, coming out as gay, deep personal stuff, their challenges, their reinventions, where they lived as children, starting a business and how to maintain it. They weren't born with silver spoons. They had to persevere. Valentino said, "I've never told an audience all this about my life!"

I'm working on new seasons of Fashion Icons talks and have two more books to produce of these illuminating interviews. These books represent my latest reinvention, and it's been a great honor to share these remarkable stories from the most influential and important designers and industry professionals.

Reflection on Fern's Radical Reinvention

What it takes to reinvent an entire industry is nothing short of ultraradical! And it takes a serial re-inventor like Fern. I can say I was there when it happened. I was one of those fashion editors, pre-reinvention, running around the city uptown and downtown, from star-studded show to star-studded show before the events were coordinated into one cohesive extravaganza, thanks to Fern's ingenuity, contacts, and courage. I hope you noticed that her passion for fashion shined through at an early age, and then she continually honed her skills. She is one of my good friends who I respect immensely. We are always discussing new entrepreneurial ventures we should be doing together.

CHAPTER 4

REMEMBER

"Hard times arouse an instinctive desire for authenticity."

—*Coco Chanel, designer*

Stage 4 of Your Radical Reinvention—REMEMBER

Resolution and Recommendations for:

Authenticity | Resilience | Truth | Values

WHEN I THINK of authenticity and remembering who you are, I marvel at Fern's illustrious story. She captured so many opportunities by being herself and growing from each experience. She courageously connected to people in various positions of power and grew her world of contacts to help her make monumental things happen in a luxury product-and image-dominated industry. Both are a hard sell because they're not considered "essential", whereas a service fastens to a target consumer base as a necessity.

I know how stressful those fashion shows were while scattered all over the city map. I was there as a fashion editor battling to get cabs and traffic, as you couldn't be late. Talk about stress level. Still, Fern did not compromise her truth. In fact, she defended her values, always came out on top, and is establishing a compelling legacy of getting designers to talk about their authentic selves and reinventions.

When you worked at *Vogue*, you could get a job anywhere, like *Harper's Bazaar*, which was my next move for a few years as senior fashion editor and then beauty and health director. Emmy Lou, my NYC roommate and still great friend, also departed from *Vogue* to go with her friend and mentor, Carrie Donovan to *Harper's Bazaar*. We both followed Carrie. This was the glossy print publication era. Any content was possible between the satin pages. But the pages weren't changing salaries or creative models enough for me to stay forever. I wanted more. The Bond Girl ambition in me wanted to be more financially independent. The entrepreneurial fever hit.

I became a spokesperson for brands like Dove and Clairol and introduced P&G's beauty division with a large fashion show in Cincinnati to the entire company. I worked with a lot of big brands. I would appear on local TV, radio and newspapers talking about what was trending in beauty products, fashion, and wellness. I only knew print, but I wanted to understand TV and newspapers and how a big idea and storytelling played a role. I would travel around the country going to the early TV morning news shows then to the local newspaper in the morning, then be on the local noon news TV show talking about trends and all sorts of beauty/fashion-related topics. They paid me an exorbitant amount of money to devote two days every other week to promoting their products, because I had other ongoing consulting. I was positioned as a beauty, fashion, and health expert because of my magazine experience. The beauty industry continues to be fiercely competitive today. Nobody taught me how to be a TV spokesperson. I had to reinvent myself. As an editor, I knew how to craft content, so I shaped my TV segments around three major points I wanted to talk about, integrating the brand more as editorial than as a paid spokesperson. It was seamless. I loved TV and it was a natural for me. They needed content, particularly for women, and developing stories around trends and products is what I did as an editor. They needed me for content/storytelling, and I needed them for experience and exposure. This consulting formula carried me through for three or four years before starting a family became my greatest joy.

Now, you have to say you're a "paid spokesperson" for each brand, eliminating liability, particularly in the pharma space. I was an instinctual visual storyteller. This was an aspect of my experience, plus guts, confidence, and good fortune. And I'm comfortable saying I wanted to make money, so I could take care of myself and live the life I had imagined. I knew my worth. Many women are reluctant to talk about money, value and worth. That has to stop.

This transition was not easy switching from print editorial, leaving a big brand and respectable company, to becoming a high-paid spokesperson to an unpaid entrepre-

neur. I was suddenly all on my own when I started Lippe
Taylor, a NYC public relations agency, without a paycheck
or any security. It was a risk, but one I had to take. If you
are thinking you don't have direct experience for your radical career reinvention, remember Fern Mallis's point about
"taste level" applying to several industries as one continuum of her career. She connected the plot points of her
career, including the wild turns. Are you sure your skills
from a previous role or passions do not translate to the next
venture? You may need someone else to validate that translation. Try. Don't think about the downside. Over-prepare.
Do research. Data is critical. Have guts and tenacity. Be
creative and strategic. Make a list of top companies you love
and go after them. Use your contacts from college, sorori-
ties, your parents' friends and of course, business experience.
Be fearless! You have to work very hard and smart to get that
first job or client and keep it. They don't come easy. Digital
word of mouth spreads fast.

Here is where the real you, whether as a return to values
or complete renewal, attaches to reinvention and sustains it.
You *reviewed* the catalyst for getting you here, *recovered* (a
gift in itself), and are *reawakened*, imagining all the possibilities. Possibilities will activate performance when you are
certain. Certainty will surely meet fear and other obstacles,
but the more you are grounded in your core, your humanity, the better chance you will thrive.

Intuitive healer, success coach and transformational
speaker Keiya Rayne, has shared her Radical Reinvention
on stages and other vehicles worldwide, and has served an
eye-popping list of clients on their own reinvention journeys. She advocates that reinvention—let alone Radical

Reinvention—is not possible without "the knowing" of authentic self. She believes in getting to the bottom of who you are and why you are here so you can tap into the profound and lasting changes from your reinvention.

Born in the Bahamas to Haitian parents who placed her in a home with a chance for a better life until they could become more stable, Keiya was molested by three generations of men (grandfather, father, son) from the age of eight to sixteen. But she had this knowing that while they could touch her body, they could not touch her soul. Even though at the time she didn't understand what that was, the knowing was the catalyst for reinventing herself. It stayed in her. Later, far from that house in New York City, alone to sift through the damage and consequently, low self-esteem, that *knowing* was a thread. Lying on the bathroom floor at 3:00 a.m. in a flood of tears after trying to commit suicide with pills, she heard a subtle voice that said, "Keiya, you were put on this earth for more than suffering. Get up!"

She did and felt like a different person. She felt a sense of peace come over her. Then she embarked on the most extraordinary journey of self-discovery, healing, and divine connection. She became much more intentional in every thought, word, and action. Along the way, she found the love of her life, Victor, became a teacher, coach, humanitarian, and sought-after speaker. As a co-founding member of Medical Wings, Keiya has been in the field, bravely providing medical aid and empowerment to isolated regions of the world. She received a United States President's Volunteering Award for her relief work during 9/11. And so much more.

Keiya now credits her mental, physical, and sexual abuse as the training ground that developed her mastery in helping others transcend their life challenges.

For true reinvention to take place, you need to connect with that energy and spirit within you, she insists. "We're here to consistently reinvent ourselves. We're limitless beings and cannot reach our full potential only by doing. High-achieving women have all the success in the world, but they come to me because they are in conflict. They've done so much to get where they are, but getting to their next level of reinvention requires them to learn how to *be*, which is often the missing link, and my work guides them in doing just that. If we don't reinvent ourselves to align with our truth, our identity is in conflict—leading to illness, unfulfilling relationships, unfulfilling lives. You're here to evolve. See reinvention as evolution. The key is to leave no stone unturned to connect with the truth of who you are. You do this by connecting with a force greater than yourself. It doesn't matter the title of that force—energy, spirit, soul, God, devote yourself to a daily practice meditation and the miraculous gift of gratitude, then witness as the universe gives you signs of how connected we truly are. If you do not 'connect' in this way, something will always be missing, and you will feel unfulfilled because the reinvention did not come from the right place. When you do connect, you gain more confidence of this existence, and then you're operating at a higher vibration that attracts so many incredible people and opportunities. Desire to change is not enough. Once you identify what you want to reinvent, you must 'get off the floor'. If I didn't follow that bread crumb, that voice, nothing would have changed. It would have remained a desire. Once you prioritize reinvention, you must give the attention and energy it needs. The greater the outer experience and desire, the greater the inner work that must be done first."

I watched Keiya's riveting and flawless TEDx and knew I had to include her insights in this book! She started her reinvention by acknowledging the knowing inside of her. Sometimes we're not mature or old enough as in her case to put forth the effort that knowing demands. Then her darkest hour on that floor brought forth the invitation, the illumination. Wow…just wow!

In the process of aligning with my truth and doing the inner work, I had to get clear on my values again. Values cannot be challenged. They have to be written in stone in your head. We are tested every day. Before we go any further, this is a good time to consider your values. They may have altered as a result of the disruption you experienced. In fact, it's likely. During COVID-19 quarantine, for example, were you more creative or did you binge it up on Netflix, booze, and bonbons? "Problem drinking" went up by 14% in 2020 in the United States alone. Did you reach out to family members over Zoom for the classic screen reunion, or did you sleep more? Did you tap into your consciousness to feel around for how happy or unhappy you were with normal life, after all? Or maybe you had always wanted to work at home with your fluffies and furries, but never had permission to. Personally, it scares me that young people with little to no experience would rather work at home alone. You will never learn being by yourself. You need to get into an office, feel your community, build friends, and learn, learn, learn. Work in an office is fun and inspirational and it's where all the learning and innovation comes from. The office is where you meet and learn from senior people, peers, as well as from clients and just doing the work together as a team. The office is where it is all happening. No human is an island. It is your community. If you're young, starting out and you want to be successful, get into the office. Join to learn. We have an epidemic of loneliness. Connection is critical. Lots to chew on from these basic thoughts.

Here is an important list of values. Identify five to ten that comprise and are authentic to you, and by the time you've closed this book, narrow it to five. If you then build your choices, decisions, relationships, routines around that center, you will be unstoppable!

Family	Hope	Inclusion
Ethics	Risk Taking	Trust
Empathy	Freedom	Forgiveness
Courage	Honesty	Perseverance
Balance	Innovation	Order
Wealth (Equity)	Creativity	Vision
Fairness	Ambition	Beauty
Loyalty	Optimism	Self-Respect
Integrity	Kindness	Independence
Resilience	Power	Dignity
Equality	Harmony, Caring	Adventure
Joy	Legacy	Pride
Inclusion	Intuitive	Inspiring

Dysfunctional or Amiable? Get Clear on the "F" Word

Did you choose *family* as a top value? It's always been mine. When I received four more pieces of new business in my new PR agency in my apartment, I didn't have a business plan. I didn't have staff. I didn't have an office. I didn't have capital. I had experience and courage only. My husband had said, "You are not set up for success. You can't do everything yourself. You have to find help. Hire your mother!" Problem solved. She was capable and open to reinvention herself, as my dad had passed in that year. But would she want to work out of my apartment with her grandson crawling around? I wooed her over lunch, and I remember her expression when she beamed, "When do I start?"

I was shocked, as my mother had a glittery job in the fashion industry in New York City, which she loved, and had many friends in the business. I never thought she would give it up to come with me and my baby to join a startup. She was a natural and endlessly pitched editors, and they fell in love with her easygoing, loving manner and charm. She was irresistible over the phone, which led to many in-person meetings and subsequent wins. She reinforced the importance of engaging interactions and intimate experiences, and passion for what you're doing, which Lippe Taylor is still known for. It's so much about relationships.

My mom joined the firm and several years later, I talked my husband, who had been publisher of *The National Lampoon*, *Harper's Bazaar* and *Spy Magazine*, into joining and not taking the big publishing job he was offered, which involved a lot of travel. It is thanks to Jerry Taylor that the company grew steadily every year and continues to grow thirty years later. He gave me the counsel and the stability to work hard and to work smart. He taught me everything I know about sales and selling. I now had my mom and my husband working for the agency. And then years later, my son joined the company to drive innovation and growth. They were Lippe's and Taylor's, and their names were on the door. This was a family affair. What a lucky girl I was to be surrounded by family, the people I trust most.

Your family of origin has a considerable impact on your development. It's called *generational fixed beliefs* and they can limit your life. As many studies can attest, your family of origin helps to shape your worldview, determines how you relate to and interact with others, and has a big effect on your mental and even physical health. These influences will impact you. The way you were raised affects aspects of your future, even if indirectly or passively. That's why it's often helpful to consider your family of origin if you're working through trauma, mental health concerns, or similar issues that may weaken, wreck, or even improve your reinvention.

Identifying the stories and beliefs you carry as a result of your family of origin will help you exponentially work through change, let alone a Radical Reinvention. So many people hold back from their dream jobs because of an ancient belief that you won't be successful if you don't attend a top college, don't make money doing what you love, or if you do, you won't love it anymore. Or it cheapens the luster. I will say this limiting belief is ass backwards. If you are skilled at something and you love doing it, and you can make money, why in hell would you put off such happiness? Examining who your parents, grandparents and siblings, or other influential family members were as real people and in relationship to you does not have to be a heavy psychodrama series here. However, you may find that seed of an answer for why you're not feeling, thinking, or living according to who you truly are. Check your beliefs and know where they came from. Create your own; don't let the family beliefs lead you.

Take my own family story as a vehicle for identifying your own. Trust me, it makes a difference for reshaping and deciphering if your values are indeed, your values, or leftovers from a family feast of teachings.

I had stable, loving, and honorable parents. I do remember this every day of my life. My mother was a model for years and then she worked at top fashion brands as head of sales. She was beautiful, affectionate, smart, and very supportive. A great mother, great cook, gardener, storyteller, funny, from Ireland. She was my friends' mother, my boyfriends' mother. Everyone loved her. She had enormous influence on me. My dad worked at Seagram's on Park Avenue and retired at sixty-four. I worshipped him and we were 'thick as thieves.' That is when I got into consulting and could spend good amounts of loving and hilarious time with my parents. They were fixtures in my life and my business. My father would say, "I'm going to pick you up right now, I need a Maureen fix!" He would drive into the city with his Alfa Romeo. I would hear the rev of the engine and know he was downstairs. Pure joy. When you have wonderful parents who love and respect you, are not judgmental, you're 60 percent there wherever you're going. My brothers, Billy and Michael, were my best friends and my protectors throughout my life. We would speak almost every day. I loved them deeply, helped them when I could, and we all lived up to our shared expectations. I did everything I could to make them proud. I have a hilarious family and we all value humor so much. Humor will take you a long way on your reinvention journey. Laugh and be well!

When I learned that my father had five weeks to live because of melanoma, this was the day I became an adult. Grief wasn't new to me when my husband died. When both my parents died, it was devastating. You do feel abandoned like an orphan. The pain is numbing. All you can do is focus on what you can control.

My brother, Billy, my warrior and rock, died of pancreatic cancer a few years ago. At the same time, he was struggling with pancreatic cancer, my younger brother, Michael, came to visit us and stay with me for Christmas. He called the night before his arrival to tell me he had cancer. I urged him to just come right away, and I would take care of everything, including his clothes. I found the doctors who would treat them both and I would sit with my two brothers telling funny stories together while they were getting their chemo at Sloan Kettering. I was honored and grateful to be the family caretaker for medical issues. What a privilege. About one year later, my best friend, Yates, died of pancreatic cancer, which was devastating. I took him to Sloane Kettering too. He had four months. I lost a lot of my vigor in those few years.

Fortunately, I love medicine and am the most frustrated doctor. When you adore your parents and brothers, meet the love of your life, and end up marrying that love, have extraordinary friends what a LIFE, but with cancer and dying, it hurts deeply and forever. What gets you through is your spouse, your partner.

You can feel my vivid family portrait of love, health, taking care of each other while keeping my business going, and most importantly, loving and sustaining my darling son, Nick. I must reiterate the substance of my life has always aimed to be authentic, and it started early with my positive relationships with my parents, brothers, grandparents, and cousins, which aligned with my reinventions. Now, in this Radical Reinvention of losing my spouse of almost forty years, I don't have all the deep and trusting family and friends I once had around me for comfort and strength. Many are gone; that's life. It's painful. Thank God for my son, Nick, my brother, Michael, my nanny, Remy, and my chosen friends and most supportive family. Between family of origin and chosen family, it is imperative to evaluate these relationships for reinvention alignment. And most importantly, I go to work and have deep and loving relationships with my colleagues, some who've been with me fifteen to twenty years. My work sustains me intellectually and emotionally and keeps me centered during this more difficult stage of my life without my partner.

Weatherly Camacho, LPC, MAC is a psychotherapist located in Savannah, Ga. who helps people to disconnect from toxicity and reengage with peace and well-being. She provides guidance on healing from trauma and transitioning from a lifestyle of surviving to thriving. With a focus on self-reflection and examination, her therapeutic approach is designed to bring unconscious behaviors into awareness so that those in her care can operate more intentionally and less reactively. Yep, she is the perfect aid on the topic of *best you*! Consider her unique take and advice as you tether to your truth. Gauge your relationships and if you need to start creating boundaries in order to make room for what you need. All your choices—how you spend your time and who you spend your time with—point to Brand You. Do they all measure up? Will you need to invent new features or as Camacho will discuss, reclaim what is already inside you? No one else in the world can define that truth for you, and you're going to need it for the subsequent attitude and actions of your Radical Reinvention.

Camacho says, "As children, we are born with pure truth: complete authenticity. We are a blank slate with the purist of hearts. Then through a series of painful experiences and trauma, combined with the harmful messages of our caregivers, even the most well-intended caregivers can pass harmful messages onto their children, we develop coping skills as a means of survival. As life goes on, and these coping skills begin to cause us harm in our adult relationships and with ourselves, we come to feel completely lost and drowning in unhappiness. We have nowhere to go but inward. What many call 'reinvention' is actually a *reclamation*. We learn who we are, and we reclaim our lives, for us. "Being performative is not sustainable in any circumstance. Whether in a relationship, friendship, work or otherwise, eventually the performance falls as we become more lost; this is what we call *burnout*. Professionally, we are finding that people are tired of having to be someone they are not. We no longer desire to spend our lives unhappy and inauthentic...merely surviving.

"The longer we live in a survival state, the louder our behaviors become. When we experience fatigue, exhaustion, or a perceived threat to wellness, our nervous system begins to fire, and we kick into survival mode. It looks frantic, robotic, chaotic, and sometimes primal. To reclaim balance, you must step outside of survival mode, and that requires boundaries. In some relationships, things can become more difficult as you introduce boundaries. There is an adjustment period where people who knew you as you *were* have to get acquainted with who you now *are*.

"Many people carry shame and judgment for who they were in survival mode. It doesn't make sense and so they feel embarrassed by their actions and choices. The flaw in this logic is that they are looking at those behaviors through the lens of today's logic, so yesterday's behaviors are not going to make sense. You did the best you could with what you had at the time.

"The most fundamental lesson that I try to communicate with all my clients is the biology of survival mode. Your brain does not care about social norms. Your brain does not care about tact. Your brain does not care about self-respect or value systems. Your brain cares about survival. The severity of the behavior is equal to the severity of the perceived threat you are experiencing. Your body will always tell you when you are unsafe—most often, our nervous system knows something is wrong before we do. When we listen to our body, we can feel when something is wrong or when we need boundaries. The decision to ignore this feeling is what we call *self-abandonment;* it's the moment we disregard our wellness for someone else. *Self-retrieval* happens when we prioritize our health and develop the boundaries necessary to protect it. Believe me, the only people who are bothered by your boundaries are those who are not interested in your well-being.

"A core principle in my practice is that we don't have to become someone we're not for anyone. In fact, we are already the person we are striving to become! All that is necessary is for us to strip away our defense mechanisms and learn who we are so that we can act with intention. We are already the person we dream of becoming—they are just buried under pain, sorrow, and shame. The choice to heal means to reclaim your life so that you can see how truly magnificent you are, naturally. A balanced life is a thriving life. Learn your truth for you. Not only do you deserve it, but so do those around you who truly love you."

It's wonderful to remember that Radical Reinvention is also a return to parts of ourselves, as Camacho illustrated. Not everything has to be redesigned. That we can take control after a disruption spun us out of control. We can declare what we need. We must—no matter what others' reactions may be. This is the heartbeat of thriving rather than surviving in self-abandonment mode. It takes truth and resilience.

Reinvention Requires Resilience...A Lot of It!

Being a caretaker is part of life, but not everyone can do it or wants to do it for their family or friends. For me, it was a measure of love and resilience, two values I most respect. Let's talk about the fusion of disruption and resilience because your own level of resilience may never be measured without disruption.

Called 'The Reinvention Guru' (*Venture Magazine*) and 'The Queen of Reinvention' (TEDx Navesink), Dr. Nadya Zhexembayeva is a business owner, educator, speaker, and author specializing in reinvention. As an educator, Dr. Zhexembayeva personally contributed to the development of nearly 5,000 executives from over sixty countries and twenty industries teaching and developing via small group executive education sessions, custom-made seminars, and long-term corporate reinvention projects. "Resilience and reinvention are connected. Reinvention is the active form of resilience. We don't have a once-in-a-lifetime pandemic; we have them every week. We have some form of disruption. If it's not a pandemic, it's economic crisis. If not economic crisis, it's inflation. If it's not just inflation, it's a recession. If not that, it's a harrowing school shooting or floods, fires, hurricanes, or tornadoes. Or maybe a new boss. it's a new technology. If not a new technology, it's a regulation of some sort. If it's not a new regulation, it's a disruption of some form on a nearly daily basis; therefore, this muscle to get up and reinvent should be automated to the point like brushing your teeth."

If I look at the headlines today, disruptions are occurring in our world in every form that she is speaking of. I've already brushed my teeth—momentum!

Whitney Johnson is both a modern-day disruptor and among the world's leading thinkers on disruption. She is an expert on helping high-growth organizations develop high-growth individuals. She is an award-winning author of several bestsellers, world-class keynote speaker, frequent lecturer for Harvard Business School's Corporate Learning and an executive coach and advisor to CEOs. As a former award-winning Wall Street stock analyst, Johnson understands momentum and growth. She was an Institutional Investor–ranked equity research analyst for eight consecutive years and was rated by StarMine as a superior stock picker. In essence, she knows resilience!

She states in the *Wall Street Journal* bestselling women's leadership book, *Arrive and Thrive*, "For a lot of people, the mentality is 'I just need to survive.' That works, but it doesn't lead you to have a life that is full of happiness if you're just always surviving. We want you to get to the point where you are arriving, and you are thriving, and you are living in *that* place. You're going to have moments where you are focused on survival, but that's not your general mentality. When I hear people say, 'I will survive,' or 'I am a survivor,' that's always identifying as survivor mode. I don't think that is where we do our best work."

I would listen to the world authority on disruption when it comes to Radical Reinvention. She reminds us that a car on ice doesn't go anywhere. But a setback can be exactly what you need to get better. In mastery, you are likely in a place of being comfortable and can coast for a little bit. And/or you may feel you don't want to start over again, that it is going to be too hard. Or you're forced to do something new, and this gives you the confidence that you can because you know that a plateau can become oppressive. You're supposed to get to the top of a wave and start at the bottom of another wave. That gives you the confidence that you can do it because it's part of that cycle of growth. It's imperative to endure to make progress. Making progress is a fundamental longing that we have.

Dr. Zhexembayeva adds: "That something or someone forced you to reinvent, or you had a need, a yearning to reinvent, it doesn't matter. There is a start and a finish. And there's a project. Then we enter a norm. The norm is not predictability and certainty. The norm in terms of nature is uncertainty and constant change. Nature does not hold onto its leaves and say, 'I'm not going to let go in the fall! I worked so hard to produce these leaves and I invested so much in these leaves, and they're like my degree.' In terms of biological systems much older than us, the norm is the constant dynamic state of uncertainty and volatility. We can no longer look at reinvention as a project and we need to look at it as a process, the normal part of our lives, like taking a shower. You don't reinvent showering every time. 'Like, oh my god, I've never taken a shower in my life. What do I do? How do I do this? I don't know where to start!' Whether you do it a lot or a little, it's not an eventful, frustrating, overwhelming event in your daily life. Hopefully you have standards in what you wash first, you have standard preferred washing equipment. It won't be announced as a new project called 'Taking a Shower!' Same with reinvention.

"If it was once before a 'blue moon' project, now it is a regular washing off of whatever does not serve us. In companies, it could be products, services, markets. In human life, it could be principles, positions, routines and habits, relationships unfortunately that no longer serve us, aspirations and dreams, locations and resources, roles. We may need to let go of roles we used to play. Welcome change as the continual evolution of you. The freedom and capacity to change is a gift! I was born in the Soviet Union, under a Communist regime, and we were not allowed to practice a new religion. Here in the States, you can practice any religion you want so resistance is not ideological. It's not economic or political. Across our schools, we learned the negative message of resistance in our era, but hopefully it's changing. We no longer can afford to not be protected by resilience and reinvention. It's an ultimate shield in a world of high volatility and high speed of change."

In my humble opinion, this phenomenal expert has the science of reinvention down! She reinforces that if you have the mindset that reinvention is constant, like training for a sport or job is continual, you will be conditioned. You may ace Radical Reinvention. Don't think it will come when you're "ready". Always prepare. Always embrace change. Stay curious. Intentionality is important. If you know your values, your self-esteem and self-worth will follow.

ALINA LEE: ALWAYS REACH YOUR HIGHEST POTENTIAL

Alina Lee is a marketing law and business transactions attorney. Prior to starting her own law firm, Your Ad Attorney, where she and other attorneys fuse their life values, mission, and purpose into their flexible schedules, largely unheard of in Big Law, she was Senior Corporate Counsel at Mailchimp, a profitable tech company with millions of customers worldwide. But before all this law business, Alina was a teen golf star. At the age of sixteen, she was already on her second season on the University of Georgia Women's Varsity golf team, which was ranked No. 1. Known as a "teen sensation" by ESPN, Alina was the youngest collegiate medalist in women's golf history. She was obsessed with being No. 1—to the point that she almost died of exhaustion trying.

Having graduated from college at age seventeen and then law school at age twenty-one, Alina has gone through several reinventions already in her early thirties. Here,

Alina talks about cultivating our innate skills to reinvent and never losing sight of reaching our potential, no matter how tough the process gets.

Like other skills, your ability to reinvent strengthens.

Traits are developed in childhood. I went to fourteen schools over the course of my life. My whole life was a constant shift. You become resilient when you don't know what it's like to have a stable environment and your only choice is to sink or swim. I wanted to have friends. Every time I was thrust into this situation, I acted. I didn't shut down. We didn't have cellphones back then and it was too expensive to call friends. The sentiment was, "You'll see each other at school tomorrow!" You lose those friends because you're now in another location and there's no contact anymore. Having to do that repeatedly was always hard. Being vulnerable is the best way to connect. You're implicitly telling people you trust them, and they feel compelled to give you the same level of trust when you find the language for it. Trust grows in the small things in life every day, not the big sweeping moments. "I'm the new kid. Can you help me? Tell me where to go?"

My next reinvention was a near-death experience in a hospital dying of pneumonia. There, I decided I didn't want to be a professional golfer and realized I was miserable. All that hard work was for nothing. It suddenly didn't matter. I decided to go to law school.

Where this gets radical is when I stopped working for other big firms and legal departments and took the steps of starting my own business to break the mold of how law firms operate or how the workplace is. Today, I've never been happier in my legal practice. I've accomplished the things I set out to do. Having the freedom to create the lifestyle, the firm the way I want. It's a lot of responsibility, but I'm helping my employees have the life they want, too. This is our shared Radical Reinvention!

It's scary going into the unknown, but your life depends on it.

Whether the reinvention is changing jobs or doing whatever it is in another life area that's the hardest thing to do, you have to actively take steps to do what can make you happy—or *key*, give yourself the chance. When faced with the possibility of a happier life versus the almost certainty of an unhappier life, that risk is worth it. Your life dream is not something to compromise on. When you realize you deserve more, if you don't do anything, how can you expect change? You have to do something. You have to shake it up. Plan B or Plan C may not work, but you learn and grow.

Never give up.

I encourage my employees to figure out their life goals, what their *why* is. Then how this firm fits. How this goal can be just one small piece in a much bigger part of their life. I'm giving them the opportunity and encouraging them to do this. They inspire me and the rest of us. In one monthly team meeting, I asked everybody to share childhood photos and talk about their childhoods. I want my people to know I see them, and I don't think their work equates to them as a person. We're all reinventing ourselves constantly. It's never too late to live the life you want to live. Take ownership and responsibility. All the training I received in golf and piano taught me to keep going. In lessons, your teachers keep planting, even forcing other ways. It's not an option to give up. You can't even have that mindset if you're not hitting well—it's required to keep trying until you fix the swing, fix the way you stand, whatever. And don't give yourself that "option" of giving up. It's ongoing, continuous action. If you're not doing the action, ask yourself why. Maybe you will find something deeper, like the direction you need to take. If it's your life, your reinvention, don't give up so easily on *you*.

Experiment.

Amass resources to help you experiment. Figure out what will help you succeed. I was talking to a life coach about how amazing it would be to bring life coaches to middle schools for emotional intelligence alone. Reimagine big *and* create bite-sized goals. Feeling like you can't get there because the dream is far or overwhelming right off can be a big obstacle. Create micro-milestones so you can visualize how you get there. Then when you finish some of those, you may realize this isn't the big dream. Experiment. I was not happy in corporate life and kept having to change. I never gave up on this goal of having a happy, fulfilling career.

Reflection on Alina's Radical Reinvention

I can relate so much to Alina's early grit and fierce obsession with achievement. Then no matter what age you are when you experience it, illness is a wakeup call to reinvent because it forces you to face your mortality with guts and grit. Alina thought she had it all before she contemplated relationships and what really mattered. The maze of challenges she crisscrossed through Big Law and corporate law to then establish her own firm full of altruism and optimism makes me feel so exhilarated and hopeful. She's also helping likeminded Radical Re-Inventors in her profession. How radically awesome!

CHAPTER 5

REIMAGINE

"When I look into the future, it's so bright it burns my eyes."

—*Oprah Winfrey,*
MEDIA MOGUL

Stage 5 of Your Radical Reinvention—REIMAGINE
Resolution and Recommendations for:

Ideas | Excitement | Illumination | Aspirations | Invention

IF YOU AREN'T inspired to Radically Reinvent after hearing the profound stories of others, perhaps reimagining will entice. If your Radical Reinvention incorporates body transition as Samantha Lux's did, for example, consider that she had to spend a lot of time reimagining before she could act and embark on any physical transformation. Her resolve had to be strong. She had to see her future life, and it had to be meaningful enough to keep going. As she said, there was "no turning back" from the grand realization.

When I started Lippe Taylor, I had a baby and realized that if I didn't jump off and do my own thing, I would be turning my back on my deep desire to be a successful entrepreneur, I would never know what it takes to develop a start-up business and I wouldn't have the financial security to afford the Bond Girl lifestyle, done my way, I so coveted. What I truly wanted was to be emotionally and financially independent even though I was married to the love of my life who was a very successful publisher. I never wanted to be dependent on anyone. I always worked as a young girl in high school and paid for all my new clothes for college. I didn't have to, but it was authentically me. I can take care of myself. And I was an entrepreneur at heart who knew her value and worth and who wasn't going to compromise despite not having a real business plan in the beginning of my business...or financing. I held tight to my values, my truth, my vision of what I reimagined life could be as an entrepreneur on my own starting a new business. I could have easily gone back to the magazine world, but that was a past version and vision of me.

If you think of yourself as an invention and possess all the material to recreate a more spectacular version at this very moment, what and who would you be? Are you ready to define it? I think of the internationally recognized artist, Orlan. A woman of many self-inventions, not tied to any one material, technology, or artistic practice. She reimagines her tangible self and uses sculpture, photography, performance, video, 3D, video games, augmented reality, artificial intelligence, and robotics, as well as scientific and medical techniques such as surgery and biotechnology. Every one-woman show is a mesmerizing display, with a higher purpose of dialogue about social construct and confinement. It's art. It's also a revolving door of brave and Radical Reinvention. Yours may not need such a high-end toolkit! But do start to figure out what it does need. This reimagining business will spur you on. You need to be excited.

When a prestigious skin care client called and asked if I would like to represent them for public relations and brand recognition, I was beyond excited. I knew how to win hearts and minds, but I also knew this brand inside and out, as I used it myself and it was very complicated. You had to be a member to buy these products. There was a new team, and I was working from home with a baby crawling around. Not an official company yet. After a major in-person presentation, they informed me that they narrowed it down to three large agencies and Lippe Taylor was in the running. They said they would come to the "office" for a high-level meet-and-greet. I had to inform the woman that I worked from home. Those days, we didn't have the miles and miles of co-working space around the globe to effortlessly book to impress.

She commented, "I don't care."

Never wavering from my internal excitement, I led her into a small office in my apartment and discussed the challenges of the Erno Laszlo Skincare Collection—preferred by Marilyn Monroe, Audrey Hepburn, and Jackie Kennedy, to name a few. The client who entered my personal space with jungle gyms, toys spread all over and tripping over trampolines was none other than Sherry Baker, an icon in the beauty business and one who believed in encouraging young women to live up to their full potential, empowering them all the way. I won the business. I won because I knew this collection of products better than the marketing team, as I used it religiously. It was a cult brand and very expensive. It was new to them, and they just didn't fully get the gestalt of this brand. I had been using the products for years; everybody at *Vogue* was a Laszlo member. It is the client that started Lippe Taylor on its way, and Sherry Baker is responsible and still a friend and mentor to this day. You never forget the people who got you where you wanted to go.

I knew as an editor all the things PR agencies were not doing to excite and delight clients and media, both a lack of creativity and a lack of strategy. It was mostly smiling and dialing. When Laszlo introduced a new sun care line, we sent out to top editors an eight-foot blow-up crocodile pool float, with a leash around his neck and a sign that said, "Stop playing games with the sun!" introducing Erno Laszlo Suncare. I called these 'strategic teasers.' You can't help but see this huge pool float when it enters your office, and you can't help but smile and want to know more about the products. They were so fun, so visual, and strategic. but it was a pool float used in the sun, and you needed protection. It was not an editor gift; it was a creative and strategic message. *New York Post* did a story inquiring about these huge crocodiles entering the Condé Nast building. Our first PR on our PR company. Eliciting excitement through creativity and unimaginable teasers to accompany new products was a differentiator for Lippe Taylor and for the industry. After a few years, all the agencies were sending gifts to the editors, but without imagination or real strategy. We never sent gifts; we sent strategic teasers to break through the clutter of a beauty editor's office and send them a strong brand message so they would write about the product. As a beauty editor, I received products in a shopping bag on average thirty deliveries in one day, and they all went into a big, dark closet. It was fun to reimagine how we were going to continuously bring excitement to all our brands and delight the media and how we would sustain the momentum and generate tons of editorial. Bottom line, we were selling product by cutting through the clutter with imagination. We figured it out every time and we were one of the most innovative, award-winning agencies in the beauty/fashion/health and wellness space for many years. And we're still going strong reinventing every step of the way. We use inspiration and imagination, and that's how we win.

If excitement and innovation is not your thing, what about aspiration? Security. Newness. Adventure. Collect ideas and create a vision board that revolves around obtaining that response. This exercise works for both the response you want for yourself and your audience, whether a new employer, clientele, or even partner, as Dr. Ann Turner was not alone in reimagining who she wanted her new husband to be!

In his book, *Roar: into the second half of your life (before it's too late)*, Michael Clinton discusses how to make the second half of your life happy and productive whether retirement is in your future plans. A dear colleague, he has coined the term "reimagineers" to distinguish this large population and breaks down tactics for tackling the rewiring it takes to reinvent at any age.

The *Roar* formula is:

- Reimagine yourself.
- Own who you are.
- Act on what's next for you.
- Reassess your relationships.

Michael writes that he's "fond of asking eighty-year-olds, 'What is your favorite future?' I also find it very aspirational that he is on the constant search for role models "who are doing extraordinary things in their seventies and eighties, ignoring self-imposed ageism or the refrain that 'you are too old to do that!" He spotlights Ginny, who, at fifty-one, reimagined herself and launched On Point for College, which has helped almost 9,000 students go to college. Mickey entered the priesthood at age forty-four. Fred, former president of New York Life, enrolled in Yale Divinity School. Now at seventy-two, he writes and speaks on faith, and his website has more than a million visits. What radical reimagineers!

As I'm hyper-focused on the "re" action items of life and reinvention, my favorite paragraph in this whole roaring book may be: "Forget the words *age appropriate* and focus on *person appropriate*. Be the one who is seen as a role model for an engaged life. While we're at it, let's banish the word *retire* and call it *refine* or *rewire* instead, as many people are living extraordinary lives after they leave their main professions. Let's stop cultural and self-imposed ageism and focus on self-imposed 'growthism'. It's time to purge many of the words that try to label us, as we gain years to our lives. In the second half of life, you can have a major renaissance in who you are and how you live."

HALENA CLINE: REIMAGINING LIFE AS AN ARTIST TO SAVE HER SOUL

Halena Cline has worked as a studio artist most of her adult life. She has a gigantic studio in Cincinnati's storied Pendleton Arts Center from which she has created approximately 4,000 paintings and sculptures. Her work is known internationally and is held in many collections, such as the extensive "Book of Innocence" series rendered in blinding colors, symbols and messages of pure reinvention that comes from the experience of travel and cultural encounters, as well as escaping a cult religion. To name the group may put Halena in danger, as it is very active today with mass recruitment, so we will refrain from using an identifier.

Escaping a cult or any system that has shaped your mentality requires radical review.

It's very rare for a member to extricate themselves from this religion. Once you leave, you are either disfellowshipped or considered an apostate. With my husband and I, there were no grounds for the congregation to disfellowship us, but they needed something tangible so that we could be "disciplined". After it was noticed that we were no longer attending their meetings, two of their elders came to our house and requested that we write letters to the effect that we didn't want to be members. Had we written letters to that effect, we would be designated "apostate" and all members, then, were to shun us, including family members.

When my husband left the religion, his parents disinherited him. After both parents were deceased, his older brother restored him in the will. Disfellowshipping is a very effective tool because it results in immediate punishment (blackmail). That's why I call it a very destructive cult. People have committed suicide. Beliefs are embedded at an early age through baptism that serves as a verbal contract. The only way to leave is to become disfellowshipped or apostate. The point is you can never leave; as "Hotel California" puts it, "You can check out any time you want, but you can never leave."

Once, I believed it all, hook, line, and sinker! I was the perfect prey. I was a high school dropout, married at sixteen, had a baby at eighteen, divorced at nineteen. A single mother in a physically abusive relationship, working as a waitress, then at a dry cleaner's supply house, counting buttons. I had no friends, my sisters were all estranged from me, and it was refreshing to find something that could give me some hope. Actually, it was the hope of seeing my mother again. And I was acquiring a set of rules and direction for my life. The church became a community I could count on. I did believe that Armageddon or the end of the world was going to happen. I tried to listen to what the men had said, to abide by their rules. The flaws started appearing as my two daughters were growing up, and I identified misogynistic abuse. But I was growing, maturing too. I got my GED and took courses for art and the business of art. It was at that time I realized that I absolutely had to leave. Art brought me into more critical thinking and freedom to express. Outside of my family, who also had to endure the transformative process of finding themselves minus the many restrictions, creating art is where I wanted to spend my hours. Drawing, painting, printmaking, photography, and silkscreen. I traveled the world for materials and inspiration. What liberation!

Reimagine a new life that is exciting and brings out different aspects of you.

For a while I had danced in two worlds. I finally realized one as a fraud and the other, honest and limitless. I grew in my confidence as an artist and my art grew as well. The positive thing about the whole experience was that I was so well-acquainted with the *Bible*, I could create pieces of art using religious imagery in a paradoxical manner. I probably would never have this knowledge if I hadn't been involved with that organization; at this point, my religion is art and all the mythical references of past world cultures.

I am a very spiritual person, but not a religious person. I'm fascinated with the idea of a collective conscience, a zeitgeist that all cultures are moved by.

I had to reimagine life, and my savior was an expression of all that I had been through and learned. How can you turn your story into a wondrous continuum? Maybe it's not through art or writing, as in this helpful and hopefully inspiring book, but have you been routinely doing a hobby that could be amplified as a profession, a gig, something that others can benefit from? Your life is a work of art! Can you turn the experience of your tragedy and learnings into a service to others? What can you teach or share that could bring your reinvention full circle, from dark to light?

I don't expect the world to see, love and understand my art, but it is indeed, my tapestry of stories, my Radical Reinvention captured in a positive way. Every time I finish a work of art, fragments of regret, sorrow, fear all leave my body as the splashes of color come to life.

Reflection on Halena's Radical Reinvention

Even though there is no one definition of what constitutes *art*, through Halena's victorious story, we can feel the power of art to express, heal, make sense of our experiences, resolve conflict, and give us alternative ways to grow, reinvent and feel joy. I was blown away when Halena said she realized she was dancing in two worlds—"one as a fraud and the other, honest and limitless". This is like the precipice of many reinventions—the in-between before we cross over into another version of ourselves.

CHAPTER 6

REACH

"Only those who will risk going too far can possibly find out how far one can go."

—*T.S. ELLIOTT, AUTHOR*

Stage 6 of Your Radical Reinvention—REACH

Resolution and Recommendations for:

Confidence | Intuition | Purpose |
Actions | Goals | Commitment

EVERY DAY IN the US, women start about 849 new businesses. Forty percent of US businesses are women-owned. Sixty-four percent of new women-owned businesses were started by women of color last year. And over the past twenty years, the number of women-owned firms increased 114%. You could herald these developments as signs that the world of American entrepreneurship is, finally, becoming more open to women. But the statistics obscure a more troubling trend. For many women business owners, starting a company is a way to escape the often-unmeetable demands of corporate life. More women becoming business owners isn't necessarily trending good for the economy—or for the women themselves. They often start businesses out of necessity. Are they reaching for their dreams or survival? No judgment here, but know the realities of entrepreneurship, too, if this is your Radical Reinvention. Starting, growing, and leading a business is not for the faint of heart. It's extremely hard work and it's risky. But, what's the alternative? If you have not tasted the territory, how do you know it's for you? To start, entrepreneurs must take calculated risks every day. Tenacity supersedes exhaustion. Confidence and curiosity almost always replace judgment and aggression. Self-awareness is key. Reach! You must live bravely, lead valiantly, and dare to be successful. There's no place for fear to run the show, but it's always looming.

I had a very successful editorial career at the height of the media hysteria. Talk about comfort zone. To leave and do something different took guts and was risky, but I love living on the edge. Men owned most of the ad and PR agencies out there when I started, and women-owned businesses were dropping like flies from the dreadfully slow tipping scales. But I wanted full independence and went full speed ahead. That said, I had a successful husband encouraging me all the way. It's not always that easy for women on their own with families to support. I had an advantage.

When you're a senior fashion editor or beauty and

health editor at magazines like *Vogue* and *Harper's Bazaar*, you have a big title and you're a buyer of content and storytelling. Everybody wants to get to you for potential coverage. You're in high demand because of the magazine you represent. In PR, you are the seller of products and information and it's so much more difficult to change people's perceptions of the brands you're representing. That is a big switch requiring a big reinvention. You're now on your own, with no top publication or platform supporting you. It's the big switch! You're going to the other side. Specific traits are required for that mind switch, as we've discussed.

Ben Horowitz's book, *Hard Thing About Hard Things*, describes a litany of challenges for startups. Super-fast read. When you are at the startup, you must do everything. If you sat down, looked at your phone, it would never ring. You have to create. From the buyer to the seller, you go from the one being pitched to, to the one pitching. My hard thing about the hard thing? People, operations, and resources, plain and simple.

Many of my editor friends called me and sent lots of new clients my way in the first few years of the company's existence. They helped build the company for me in the early years, as we had grown up together and we trusted each other, and they loved the creativity and excitement surrounding the company and the brands we represented. And we represented only the best brands.

Failure is transformative if you pay attention, and you critically look at why you failed. What are the key learnings? Do a post-mortem on the failure, realize you won't do "that" again and move on. Information sets you free.

This is growth. I've had my share of failures. It is critical to break down why and how to prevent them ever again. The big things in my life didn't fail; my marriage, who my son is, the beautiful family I have, my most supportive friends, the business I created. I'm proud and grateful for it all. Take the emotional reaction out of something not working. It's worse not to try. Have the discipline and perseverance to embrace it and turn it upside down and inside out. Where did you go wrong? Dispel the myth that you'll always get it right. Process and close the chapter as a key life learning. Move on! Growth is positive. Sometimes you grow and learn more with failure than you do with success because there are more lessons with failure. Failure hurts. You pay attention to hurt. The very act of trying (and "trying again") catapults your confidence level.

Consider this test for your mindset and why you may be resisting stepping into the unknowns of your reinvention. Dr. Carol Dweck coined the terms, *fixed mindset* and *growth mindset*, to describe the underlying beliefs people have about learning and intelligence. Dweck found in her research that one of the most basic beliefs we carry about ourselves has to do with how we view and inhabit what we consider to be our personality. A "fixed mindset" assumes that our character, intelligence, and creative ability are flat givens we can't significantly change, and success is the affirmation of that inherent intelligence, an assessment of how those givens measure up against an equally fixed standard. As a result, striving for success and avoiding failure at all costs become a way of maintaining the sense of being smart or skilled. But failure can be transformational, so this mindset simply doesn't work for reinvention!

A "growth mindset," on the other hand, thrives on challenge and casts failure not as evidence of unintelligence but as a prompt for growth and for stretching our existing abilities. Dweck insists our capacity for happiness and confidence can be contingent on having a growth mindset. Cultivation of a growth mindset will help you cultivate courage because it *rewards* not knowing it all. "I don't know" turns a lack of knowledge into an opportunity for personal improvement. You currently lack the knowledge or skills but you're willing to work to acquire them. This willingness springing from growth mindset allows you to walk through the doors of the unknown. When I consider this statement, I think of all my friends, Radical Re-Inventors, featured in this book, who courageously walked through the doors of unknowns with no guarantees of their reinventions. But they walked to freedom from quite challenging places they had to exit. Liz in an abusive home. Alina in toxic workplaces. Fern working in chaos when she knew it could be so much better. Samantha in a body that contrasted her identity. Halena in a restrictive, misogynistic cult.

Confidence is a better look than doubt. It shows in your leadership presence. And presence is not only worn in business. Leadership presence is part of the reinvention. Everyone comes under reinvention. How you present yourself is a learned skill. You must think about everything down to your nail polish, as Fern Mallis said she did when she started working for *Mademoiselle*. We're all in the business of sales—that sale at this crucial time might be yourself. Call it PR or communications, but you've got to get good at sales.

Freud said, "Anatomy is destiny." I don't believe it has anything to do with being beautiful. Look at someone you admire who has the "it factor", the *nerve, talent, fearlessness and charisma* (thank you, Rihanna!). It's not beauty. It's cues, looking people in the eyes. How you present your confidence. You know those earlier soapy commercials, cooing, "Don't hate me because I'm beautiful!" I never hated you because you're beautiful. I hated you because you're not living up to your full potential.

During the height of COVID-19, I was doing an interview for *PRovoke Media* with Kelly McGinnis, SVP & Chief Communications Officer at Levi Strauss. She got on screen, hair pulled back and not a touch of makeup. For me, it was a miracle that morning that I even brushed my teeth! (Sorry, Dr. Zhexembayeva.) *Do we even want to dress like that anymore? Put gobs of makeup on, give your hair some beach waves, with all these people struggling in the world?* That was the message Kelly was in sync with, the psyche of the country. She was intuitive. She was confident, she was smart, she was splendid. She was aligned to the time and climate. She could adjust and adapt. None of this is possible without confidence and authenticity.

Authenticity comes with a lot of risk for public figures, but more and more feel it's essential to come out with their truth.

Former First Lady Michelle Obama's book, *Becoming*, has sold 17 million copies worldwide because it revealed such a distinguished woman's genuineness and willingness to speak her truth and created the 'Becoming Phenomenon'. The fact that she was candid about not wanting her husband to run for the U.S. Presidency and so many other truths that mark her life and legacy resonate with the masses. Her most recent book, *The Light We Carry*, shares coping strategies for surviving stress and uncertainty, and God knows there's a lot of that going on. *The New York Times* calls her a world-class worrier, a change-avoider and by her own admission, a bit of a nervous nellie. Sound familiar? It's okay.

Also, risking their reputations and opportunities in the glossy world of film, TV and music where they are some of the most photographed and scrutinized people in the world, Bruce Willis, Lady Gaga, Jane Fonda, Christina Applegate, Serena Williams, Michael J. Fox, Sia, Selma Blair, and Selena Gomez, to name a few, have played a significant part in raising awareness about chronic health and mental health conditions with their whole hearts. We don't know if they ever feared shame, stigma, or imperfection, but they had the courage, perseverance and confidence to know they would be educating by putting a face to the illness and getting it out of the closet. Bless them all.

TRIGGER WARNING

[May evoke psychological stimulus that prompts involuntary recall of a previous traumatic experience—or downright frustration for not Radically Reinventing sooner due to the following. May evoke unintended supernatural references. I'm sorry.]

Demons: The Illogical Elements that Stay in Your Way of Radical Reinvention

If you are being haunted by one of the following demons, let's work through it together and sage the place of your existence that is experiencing the most activity. Risk taking requires uninhabited space. You need room to move in the chances you're taking. Your courage may need to be fattened up by taking incremental risks. They accumulate. We need to expel wasteful things like shame, blame, reliability and status quo, the almighty inner critic, or at least soften her up; she can be the devil in disguise.

Shame

We need to work on shame. We constantly say, "I'm sorry." See, I said it a few lines ago; I meant it that time though. We're an 'I'm-sorry culture.' The shame we feel is debilitating, and it's a useless emotion. Why do we carry this? When women had miscarriages, they almost never talked about it. They were hit with stigma and shame when they needed everyone in the community to rally around them and send them care baskets, not shame or ignore them. It's like cancer forty years ago. My grandfather had lung cancer. No one talked about it. It's very Irish to keep stoic and quiet. This applies to leadership at work and at home. When you try to reinvent, you must get rid of a lot of this baggage. You must do a clearing so you can focus on what really matters. I find myself saying sorry all the time, all day long! I have stopped saying it for the last six months, and it's become a mission to get women to lose this word in their vocabulary. It's just too easy to keep saying. STOP!

Or we tend to say, "I think" or "I mean". It's how you feel. Don't doubt, don't voice this. Words carry power. They grow into stories. As much of a wordsmith as we are, I also realize that sometimes words get in the way of action. Too much rumination, even aloud, makes Radical Reinvention shift in its seat waiting for you to act. You know what I admire Samantha Lux for the most? So young, so courageous, she did not hesitate to review and talk to her parents once she came out of any confusion about her identity. She declared the need for resources. She couldn't do it alone. And she went into the surgical theatre, which is a terrifying place before anyone even touches you. Samantha took so many risks before real experience or historical reference. She had no clue of the outcome on her body, mind, very existence. But she could no longer live in falsities and misalignment. This was an authentic call to courage and growth.

As discussed, we have imagination, ideas, vision, hope, faith, and resources, but we don't have guarantees on the other side of change. Hell yes, it requires the courage to act. The hope is that the outcome will be more blissful than your fantasy or ideal.

Inner Critic

Look no further than Susan MacKenty Brady's book, *Mastering Your Inner Critic and 7 Other High Hurdles to Advancement: How the Best Women Leaders Practice Self-Awareness to Change What Really Matters*, for the scary lowdown and promising solutions for controlling this crazed character screeching in your mind before it turns into Chuckie. Brady explains, "You may ignore it for a little while, but at your most vulnerable times, for instance, when you're feeling stressed, insecure, unhappy, exhausted, or unclear, an inner voice expresses judgment, frustration, or at its most extreme, harshness and contempt. This 'inner voice' can be instructive and clue us into some feelings or thoughts that might be helpful as we navigate life and relationships. When extreme, this inner voice can also hurl offensive assaults on us and others. Despite where the Inner Critic is aimed, the commentary is anything but happy, loving, compassionate, and curious." When this voice attempts to push you off the mountaintop of your potential, she recommends pausing and accessing your "compassionate center" as a place inside of you that you can conjure up whenever need be and return to it when you need to. It's a place of forgiveness, empathy, compassion, and humor. Just thinking of it reminds you to be gentle with whatever you're contending with. Your Compassionate Center is the part of you that takes a child in her arms whispering, "it's okay" and "I'm right here for you" when they are crying after falling off their bike. At its core, it is love. It is acceptance. It is where safety is created.

Reliability

Self-development coach Liza Andrews warns that reliability can morph into destroying a dream of your future self if it hints at being "unreliable". She explains that people who identify as 'reliable' had their identity built upon them being the ones who have been paying the bills for twenty years or taking care of others. For this population, there may be "filters" not allowing reinvention to happen. Even when they find what they are more talented in, were made for, and would be more productive and happier, they don't allow themselves to go ahead unless reinvention looks like another 'reliable' dream. You can't feel like you are doing something so outrageous, or it will not work— even if a partner supports it psychologically or financially. According to Andrews's experience, well-paid executives who reach their fifties and dream of switching gears to an artistic career see it as being irresponsible, no matter if it talks to their heart, or if they already spent decades prioritizing financial goals. "The secret is giving permission to yourself by devoting small steps to that new reality or you will keep conforming."

Andrews suggests, "If your reliability filter is containing your dream, start doing what you enjoy or want to transition to on the side. Doing your passion project in parallel with/to your solid job brings variety to your brain. Surprisingly, it will contribute to day-to-day solutions because you are now free of some of your frustrations and are also exposed to new experiences. Doing something you love on the side, or every free hour, gives you mental strength and purpose as well. I come from a family where having a serious career was primordial. We could only go to business school, medicine, or law. But I always had a strong artistic vein and decided to devote myself to both, studying literature and photography, alongside business school. I worked for the major telecommunication company in Brazil and later moved abroad to work for an American company with vast business in Europe. Those were the money-makers, the great opportunities to network and travel the world, and yet in parallel, I wrote novels and did professional photography. This gave me a full life, combining money and satisfaction.

"When you don't plan and the need for reinvention comes later in life, here's what you can do. Sometimes reinvention comes with saving some money first, retiring, creating community and a revenue generator online. Many of my clients and I identify with this type of personality that wouldn't have been able to do what we love without a 'reliable' plan. The key is believing that by planning, you can reinvent yourself at any age, even if what you'd love to do at sixty seems crazy for some who know you as the professional you are now. Life has phases, and psychiatrist James Hollis explains that it's in midlife that most people experience depression, when depression can be a lack of purpose. This is also the phase we question everything we have done and when our identities no longer match our old choices, personal or professional, it's time to change. I am glad that I kept my passion near me, despite my reliability filters, so now in my fifties, I can have solid ground to update and why not, *upgrade* my lifestyle; and without financial loss, do what brings me joy, help others in new ways, and this will be remembered as my legacy."

Liza Andrews is a "reimagineer", as Michael Clinton deems. She breaks free from the reliability factor and reaches.

With reaching as a constant part of her life, Keiya Rayne added: "Reaching is natural. We are limitless! I felt guided to change my name, not because I didn't like it, but to align with my greater potential. This wasn't a difficult choice, as I was not tied to my family or culture. I was free. Reinvention frees us from imprisonment of our culture, upbringing, society or cages we put ourselves in. The only way to break free is to reach and reinvent. Reaching is energy. Just as we get dressed and prepare to interact every day, we need to prepare ourselves energetically every day. You build intuition. We're being guided all day long, given information to support us, but if we're too busy inside of other noise, our decisions and choices can fail us. It's energy intelligence. When you master your energy, you master your life. Everything becomes hopeful and delicious."

Every Radical Re-Inventor featured in this book has had to evaluate demons, dungeons, dragons in their lives preventing them from reaching. When you come to terms with aspects of your personality, such as the reliability factor, or circumstances countering your actions for reinvention, you can identify where you may need to deposit more radical courage in your life.

ERIC ALVA: RADICAL COURAGE

THE FIRST MARINE injured in the Iraq War, Eric was hailed as an American hero. While he lost his leg in combat, his spirit remained stronger than ever—upon retirement, Eric came out as gay. As a former spokesperson for the Human Rights Campaign, he played an instrumental role in the repeal of the military's "Don't Ask, Don't Tell" policy on gay, lesbian and bisexual service members, working with members of Congress to end the discriminatory practice. As a gay man, disabled veteran, and U.S. citizen of Hispanic and Native American heritage, Eric knows about overcoming obstacles. Here, he shares how the aim of serving others helps to navigate complex reinventions.

Courage can co-exist with pain.

We can't wait for the pain to go away before we make the next move. From losing my leg in Iraq, trauma and sounds affect me. The other day, something went off and it scared me half to death. We all suffer from post-traumatic stress. Thank God for medication. I am still learning; I am still reinventing. I believe it is continual. Growth is a feature of reinvention. Mine was quite radical. I had been in the Marines for twelve years and had extensive awards, letters of appreciation and good conduct. I was the perfect Marine. I think back and wonder if I was outshining fellow Marines because I was gay and trying not to get caught. My fitness tests. My job. I believe in a sense the wars in Iraq and Afghanistan were very popular after 9/11. In 2002, with the reports of WMD [weapons of mass destruction], we went to Iraq within fifteen months of Afghanistan. We wanted justice and revenge. The citizens of this country were supportive. When I got injured, I had only been in Iraq for three hours of the ground war. I was in Basra and woke up in a dark hospital in Germany. It takes my breath away to know I had wanted to die. I thought my life was over in that hospital bed, seeing my leg missing.

When I finally transferred from a bed to a chair after being cooped up for many days, the media bombarded me before I could even breathe in fresh air. My reinvention started in excruciating pain physically, mentally, emotionally. The fresh air and sunlight reassured me that I still had a life to live. I was determined to do something powerful once I recovered.

Live your days in discovery.

In 2005, Texas passed a state constitutional amendment banning same-sex marriage and it passed overwhelmingly.

In 2006, majoring in social work, something woke up in me. Empathy, stigma, diversity, dignity, self-worth. I started to see in the midterm elections, eight states had now proposed state constitutional amendments banning same-sex marriage. I was in a relationship. He said, "With all this distinction, you need to use your voice." That fueled more discovery. I eventually introduced myself to the Human Rights Campaign and became a spokesperson to overturn Don't Ask Don't Tell. I went from having a military life, fighting for my country on the battlefield, to coming out as a gay Marine and fighting for other LGBT service people to be able to live their lives authentically.

President Barack Obama signed hate crimes bills into law. The stage was set. In 2010, at the end of his State of the Union, he declared he would put an end to Don't Ask Don't Tell. On my birthday, I got a call from the White House to stand next to the President when he announced the repeal. What an honor. I thought that would be the end of my "activism", but it was only the beginning. I talk about being gay, Hispanic, disabled, a veteran—the inter-sectionality of my life. I've been on the speaking circuit for fifteen years.

Gratitude is the glue of Radical Reinvention.

See every day as a new opportunity to learn and grow. Make this your soil to grow new life inside of you, as you. Reinvention is rewarding and exciting. Getting to the positive newness may be extremely challenging, even dark as hell, as I experienced on many nights crying myself to sleep, but I promise you, your reinvention may be the light and true life you need at your core self. Today, I am a scuba diver and a skier. I have a wonderful husband and we have a home together. I reflect, give thanks, give myself guidance daily, and give back.

Reflection on Eric's Radical Reinvention

Eric's Radical Reinvention is historical! It changed the course of history and human rights. I can only imagine the depths of pain he experienced in that hospital room in Germany, physically and emotionally, knowing his former life was over. He had no idea what lie ahead, right down to how his body would function as soon as he left the dark room that housed all his misery. Eric also shows us that losing it all doesn't have to be the end. It can morph into a beginning of the best versions of ourselves.

CHAPTER 7

REPLENISH

"Reinvention is the biggest gift I've been given. I've gone from graffiti artist to jewelry maker, urban musician to conductor."

—*GOLDIE, VARIED*

Stage 7 of Your Radical Reinvention—REPLENISH

Resolution and Recommendations for:

Finances | Resources | Independence
| Relationships | Security

CONGRATULATIONS! YOU'VE PROCESSED, felt, and thought a lot on this radically wild ride of reinvention. Perhaps you even punched out your anger on your silk goose down pillow! You lost something profound or someone sacred from your life. Time for some gains. It won't be without pain, perhaps even bone-crushing exhaustion, but the best of you will be waiting on the other side. Everyday actions speak louder than words and stories in your head. You must amass resources—finances, time, people, technology, training—and then use them appropriately.

Financial stability gives you choices and access to opportunities and opens doors. My friend, who is considering divorce, did not push herself enough professionally or financially. Now, she's trapped in this marriage. Or she feels trapped.

The CEO of Lippe Taylor just got off the phone with a big bank client who talked about a project reaching women and financial independence. He said, "Maureen needs to be on this call because it's her thing, it's her message to women all over the world." And it is my thing and my mantra! You cannot totally depend on anyone else; you must be financially and emotionally independent, as I have reiterated many times and preach to women whenever I get the chance. This reinvention is personal to me. You need to build, sustain, and personally claim your own financial freedom whether you work for yourself or someone else. And if you want to be an entrepreneur and have total freedom and control of your life, be financially independent. This is my story. It is my truth. I live it every day. It really paid off for me. It will for you, too.

If you had three children, and you don't have or gave up a successful career and your partner comes in wanting a divorce and takes the house and then wants shared custody, you have nothing. Where do you go? That should be the biggest fear of any young woman today. How do I plan my life and my financial independence for the security of me and my family? That is part of reinventing at a young age, which we should all be doing and teaching our daughters and sons to do as well. It is reinventing to just think that way, hustling, earning, saving, and investing smartly. It's not about love, sex, emotion only. First and foremost, I need financial independence. No one talks about it! I have talked about it for years to my colleagues in workshops, particularly to younger women who must start to think this way. Knowing your value, your worth, is critical and not being fearful to bring it up to your partner, your boss or your family is critical. I'm not ashamed to say I work hard, and I am proud of the money I have been able to accrue. I left editorial because I knew I would never make the money I needed for the life I wanted.

Your financial worth and security is something you have to be comfortable discussing. I discuss it all the time and I was in a loving, trusted relationship with a successful husband. I always had a separate bank account, which I just thought was smart. You cannot afford timidity in your Radical Reinvention.

"It's Important to Find Your Tribe." (RuPaul)

Money never compares to relationships in this game of life. Both are equally important, however, stacked up as the resources, the real deal, of how your Radical Reinvention functions, I can't think of such a rebranding that does not take money, hard work, strategy, and people. To start, you must figure out early: Who am I and what inspires me and brings me joy? What do I really want from a career? What's my value, and what am I worth? What is my area of excellence and the most important skill I offer? What's my dream job and what is it that I always wanted to do with my life but didn't have the confidence?

Identify what is significant and what excites you and brings happiness. DARE TO DREAM. You must take it seriously and take control of your career and your life as early as possible and figure out how to get the job you want to live up to your full potential. Target the job you'd love to have and target the company that excels in that category. Go after the job you want with all your being; it's not going to come sweeping into your home. Find people who can help make connections for you and discover who the important people are at your identified companies and develop a strategy to get to them, and creatively reach out to the HR staff. Do something that makes you stand out. You must seriously think and plan on how to increase your earning potential beyond your expectations. You must have confidence in yourself and fearlessly just go for it. You have nothing to lose. Take risks and take personal responsibility to figure out where the big career and money opportunities are in the areas that excite and delight you. Also, think about advancement. In what fields can you quickly move up the career ladder and continuously increase your earning power, as well as your passion and joy?

I know this is challenging and can be terrifying at times, but if you want job satisfaction, personal wealth, and real success, you must think of all these opportunities and follow your heart, but most importantly, follow the money. In other words, what drives your passion and how can you monetize that for the life you always dreamed about? Don't be afraid to take risks or move to another city if there is opportunity for you somewhere else. Read business books, websites, or online publications in the areas you are interested in. Get to know the category inside out and the leaders in each field. Follow them. Write to them. Step up to the plate and design the most profitable and enjoyable reinvention possible. Remember my *Vogue* story and how I failed at first. I had the confidence to go back and try one more time. I have been living off that job experience for all my working life. It was a first job out of college and the *Vogue* brand carried a lot of weight. Top brand companies when you're starting out can take you far. You are 100% responsible for the life you want to live. Who's your Bond Girl?

Don't forget the woman with three children whose partner wants to take the house and could get the kids as well. I've worked with hundreds of women and have friends who have had horrific experiences. This storyline is prevalent. Be aware. Plan now. Don't be a victim. Be smart. Be fearless. Keep your own bank account separate to secure your financial future. Take complete control of your life, your career, and your money to protect your future. Know that these steps in no way take away from a relationship or love and union with another—they are acts of self-love, independence, destiny, and holistic care essential to the individual journey. They are also qualities to be admired and respected by a partner, I would argue. I don't mean to preach, but this is important.

During COVID-19 when our workplaces were turned upside down and we were all trying to stay connected, I thought about our younger staff in tiny New York City apartments, alone and without their family members. I was worried day and night about their health, isolation and mental wellness and would try to stay connected to as many as possible each day. We set up therapy sessions for anyone who needed counseling. Their mental wellness was more important than their professional wellness. If they are falling apart at home, living with fear and loneliness, we have to take care of them. We must be all those things for them. This is our community. We are a 'people first' company and our low turnover proves this point. We were very concerned about mental fitness and emotional wellness because our people were producing at such a high level, and they were living in the uncertain COVID-19 world. Connecting with them as frequently as possible was a management priority. Several days a week, we would have hour-long 'Refresh & Recharge' breaks when you couldn't be on your computer. Time for a mental rest. We also banned meetings on Friday. We had 'happy hours' constantly on Zoom together. Anything joyful to bring us together. Initiatives designed for mental and physical wellness plus connectivity is mandatory still.

We recently surveyed our staff again. They are happier people. Many feel they belong to a special community, are listened to, and belong to a close-knit tribe. To build a culture of inclusion and engagement, we have developed many ERGs (employee resource groups) in which people of similar interests, faiths, culture, gender come together and meet regularly to feel meaningful connection. It includes areas of leadership, culture, and inclusion. They are internal communities of workers with shared identities and interests. Anyone with like-minded colleagues is encouraged to start an ERG. This has been a successful initiative for our people to bond with each other and share their culture with the staff. We care about every one of our people and hopefully they know it. DEI (diversity, equity and inclusion) has been a top priority for our company with the mandate to promote an overall safe, welcoming workplace environment for those of all races, creeds, and ethnicity. It is a continuous mandate and challenge to keep getting better. To not lose our people, we have to protect them—all of them. We never mandated that people come to the office; we suggested two days a week for now. We have close to 250 people.

A pandemic is the radical disruption. If you are a business leader today, you must show empathy, courage, transparency, vulnerability, and strength. You have to be there for your team 24/7 building trust every single day and connecting across the organization as often as possible. You have to care for the people you hope to trust. Loyalty is critical and it goes both ways. In our staff meetings during difficult times, I would encourage our people to call me anytime. I conduct daily calls and in-person meetings to just check in and hear what's troubling my colleagues or what's working well for them, plus what we could be doing better for them at Lippe Taylor. Listening is imperative. It's been a tough and unstable time for us all. A calm, healthy and stable environment is important. Putting our lives back together takes time. It's hard but so worth the struggles and emotional connections. As they say in the military, "Embrace the suck!" I feel this is a big part of my purpose to encourage and listen to our people and preserve our culture so we can engage together in change and move forward. People want to and deserve to be heard and feel they are valued.

Who will you call for help during your Radical Reinvention? Who will you seek for trusted advice? Share tears. A loan. A skill. Some people get paralyzed when they have to make a change, yet human beings are designed to change, to move. You may also be designed to mentor others even when you don't see your assistance and uplifting of others as *mentorship*.

It is an honor to be invited to serve on an executive board. Almost every board I have served on has been about mentoring women and girls in underserved communities, including homeless shelters where we came in monthly to instruct women how to look the part to find jobs in order to get their families out of the shelters. Instructions included how to look professional, how to interview, how even to shake someone's hand, look them in the eye and state their name. Sounds simple, but for many, it's excruciating due to such low worth and self-esteem. We would practice this repeatedly. We brought in the best beauty pros in the business to teach them about the importance of looking professional and living up to your full potential. We would leave beauty products for them in all those categories to keep on hand for potential interviews for employment and for their own enjoyment.

Helping women and young girls have better lives has always been my authentic purpose and service. I'm presently a board member of the Step Up Women's Network, mentoring, advising, and reiterating the importance of a college education and how to navigate the destination—wherever that destination may be. This is an amazing national program I am honored to be serving. On the board of The Women's Venture Fund, I helped young women entrepreneurs secure loans to start their businesses. It was thrilling to get the call that they had received funding. Frequently, I would hire them myself to give them extra money until they got funding.

The original makeover program at the WIN (Women in Need) shelters, which I co-founded, lasted many years, visiting five shelters once a month accompanied by top makeup, hair, skincare, nail pros in the industry from companies like Maybelline, Clairol, CND, who were all my clients at that time. We would rotate services every month dedicated to different areas of interest so women would not participate in the same workshop more than once. A van would take us all to the Bronx and Brooklyn shelters. We would gather the product, gather the volunteers, fill the vans and off we went to see our friends in the shelters and their darling children who we loved. We even brought special volunteers in to take care of the children while we worked in another area to help the moms get ready for their sessions. We were never sure who would show up each month at the site of the vans. This program involved CEOs, top marketing execs and assistants alike— anyone who wanted to be part of this amazingly successful venture that was written up in *The New York Times* and *New York Post*. Even my young son, Nick, would come along at times and play with the kids. I wanted him to understand the importance of service and purpose. The entire beauty industry supported this program. The women in these shelters needed to get jobs. Clothes were donated. We would tress and dress them, teach presence and confidence to better prepare them for future employment. *Glamour* magazine sponsored women's breast health self-examinations and would come in with prosthetic breasts to demonstrate what an actual breast lump felt like to the human touch. We were all learning. This program lasted for years.

These were unbelievable shelter reinventions. WIN (Women in Need) working with CEW (Cosmetic Executive Women) provided essential resources to help these women living in shelters with their children to figure out what was required to build confidence, look the part, practice interview skills, and secure a job...start a new life outside a shelter in a home. Most importantly, they felt respect and special for a few hours every month and never marginalized. We created a safe space for them inside the shelter. Every girl loves to play with makeup and hair products and leave with bags of goodies. Who doesn't love a makeover?

Starting a new life after leaving an abusive home or living in a shelter is ultraradical, as Liz G. Bailey courageously showed us. Starting this program and executing it was one of the most impactful and important initiatives I had the privilege to participate in, continuously feeling the joy of real purpose and service. I loved these women and their children.

My son watched me and his dad as dedicated, loving parents, but also, as business leaders all his life. Since I started Lippe Taylor in our apartment when he was a baby, he knew hard work and success was integral to both of his parents. He also understood how relevant purpose and service was to us both and saw many examples of commitment towards helping those in need particularly. His dad served on the board of Phoenix House for over twenty years working with kids and adults who were addicted to drugs and alcohol. It was the 'Just Say No' program that Nancy Reagan supported. When he was in college, Nick traveled to Mumbai to work on a documentary set in a "Slum Dog" like school. He fell in love with these kids and really wanted to return and help them in some way that could enhance their life and give them a chance. Upon returning from India, he shared that he had a tremendous passion to return. Upon completing college, he went back to the same Mumbai school having secured a position on his own to teach the children English and math. Nick lived there for almost a year both teaching and lovingly connecting every day and many evenings with his kids. I went to visit him for three weeks to experience his world with the children he adored, and we traveled through his India. When he returned home, he financially committed to support the school with the little money he had at that time. The point of this story and journey is to remind you that our children are sponges of good and evil. They are observing us every step of the way. Nick saw how his parents lived their lives and he closely followed us in his desire to live a life with purpose and service, spending almost a year in a very hot and sometimes dangerous city to so passionately and lovingly teach some of the poorest children and families on the planet. He was the happiest boy for those months spent with his kids and would frequently visit them at their homes in the slums of Mumbai. Set the example and they will follow.

When Nick returned from India, he asked me point blank, "Mom, how can I help you in your business?" He has been at Lippe Taylor ever since. He has been a constant partner who I trust completely and who brings innovation, a different and modern perspective and growth to the business.

Nick said, "My mom is someone who doesn't look for permission to do things. A powerful executive when there weren't a lot of females in these positions, and she was not waiting for things to get better for women. She paved her own way and hired and inspired hundreds of women along the way. She was empowered before 'women's empowerment' became a thing. She braved her own trail, fearlessly and with extreme confidence. She really didn't need a movement to support women. She's always been a 'movement.' She never liked the term 'boss lady' or 'lady boss' because you shouldn't have to distinguish yourself as a woman when you have the power and are the boss. It should be self-evident there are female bosses and male bosses, and both are equally important and to each other, as advisors and mentors.

"A lot of people slam the James Bond movies saying they objectify women, but if you watch the newer ones, the women are kicking as much ass as James himself. My mom loved those movies, and they inspired her at a very young age to work hard and smart and strive for success and financial security and feel equal to the boys. They showed her what was possible in life for women, a life many young girls didn't know existed."

It's true. You already know the Bond Girls are among my early role models and mentors. My two brothers introduced me to the franchise, and I was never the same. James Bond is still reinventing and rebranding as we speak, reports Ray Ampoloquio for *xFire*. For those of you not *as* familiar as me with the Bond enterprise, it's worth noting that James Bond is a cinematic staple after Sean Connery first starred as the suave and debonair secret agent James Bond in 1963. The most recent actor to play him and the most commercially successful one is Daniel Craig. The fifty-four-year-old actor first portrayed James Bond in 2006's "Casino Royale" and ended his run with the release of "No Time to Die", which set a then-record global box office take of $733 million, according to Ampoloquio.

The first Bond Girl that made such an impression on me was Ursula Andress's portrayal of Honey Ryder in the now iconic scene in "Dr. No" in 1962 where she steps out on the beach with the swagger and determination of a tough and skilled warrior. Since then, there have been Bond Girl villains, allies, and girls who accomplish both. As of this writing, Ursula is eighty-two and still looking fierce. No ageism with the Bond Girls. I also loved "Pussy Galore" from Goldfinger in 1966 played by Honor Blackman. She passed in 2020 at ninety-four. I wonder what Radical Reinvention she may have embarked on during her lifetime. And Jill St. John played diamond smuggler, "Tiffany Case", in "Diamonds Are Forever" in 1971. Talk about resources!

"Bond Girls Are Forever" is my mantra in my world of superheroes and mentors, as they were smart, confident, cunning, strategic, resilient, athletic and could always stand up fearlessly to the male villains and characters, including James. They were beautiful, smart, powerful, fierce, and oh, so dangerous! In the early years, they were extremely sexy and used their sex and beauty to get what they wanted, but have evolved dramatically. The Bond

Girls looks eclipsed their character's sex for intelligence, confidence, and wit, and were never damsels in distress. They related to men watching the movies, but they also related to me in a very powerful way. They were stimulating, adventuresome and travelled all over the world doing all sorts of dangerous and provocative things. I related to the economic freedom and the money it took to carve out a life like that for myself. Remember too, Bond Girls frequently have the same profession as Bond. So many people would rather think the girls have no understanding or power in Bond's mission. Don't forget that at least six Bond Girls were undercover government agents. Most people come away focusing on these women's looks, disregarding the fact that they have had similar experiences as Bond, and are the female version of him. In the more recent Bond films, they distance themselves from sexually objectifying women, which is significant as it signifies that the more modern 2000 Bond films are the more contemporary and who understand their followers see the women in a much more equal, complex, and powerful way. If you feel the girls are being objectified, so too must you understand that the same happens to James. It is all so mysterious and wonderful and it's why the Bond Girls are still my heroes and had a huge impact on who I wanted to be like and the exhilarating life I wanted to lead when I grew up. I also realized I would have to work hard and smart to be able to pay for that lifestyle. That fact never left me to this day, and it inspired me to be an entrepreneur. My only regret as I look back is that diversity should have been more prominent in the girls and that was a casting flaw in the early years but was remedied in the later movies. That said, the girls always knew their value and their worth and how to live up to their full potential. They never had to demand equity. For me it was not about their beauty, but about their brains and ability to have a mysterious and exciting life that took them all over the world.

What better role models could a young girl like me have in those early days? It never would have been Taylor Swift, Katy Perry, or Ariana Grande. Maybe Lizzo, Rihanna, or Lady Gaga. I was a NYC girl and thought I was way too smart and fierce to relate to pop stars. I love my Bond Girls and still want to be one someday.

For the record, since I've been asked, Marvel's female superheroes don't appeal to me in the same way. They don't seem real or as relatable. However, I do love and admire "Sarah Connor", played by Linda Hamilton in "The Terminator" franchise. She is a favorite who is meant to introduce a woman destined to save humanity from the machines. She is a tribute to the strength and courage of women, but I knew when I saw the movies, I couldn't save humanity. I could, however, build a stronger, fiercer body and smart mind like Sarah, and that was important and inspiring.

Another great character I loved was "Ellen Ripley", played by Sigourney Weaver in the "Alien" series. She was so tough, so smart, so emotional, but never vulnerable and could seriously fight huge monsters. Her transformation and progression over the course of the four movies was powerful. Legend has it that the character was written for a man, which makes it even more interesting. I loved and revered both these female superheroes but couldn't see myself in either role. I didn't strive to be them; it was too much of a stretch, but I admired them, and they remain two of my favorite movie characters. Ironically, both characters were directed by James Cameron.

You can find marvelous mentors and role models in books and movies. You don't have to party with them every day to resonate with their skills, their power, prowess, and presence. You're resonating with what they personify or represent to you and your future self and state, your Radical Reinvention.

Ask yourself if you need a mentor, teacher, life coach, therapist, support group, wellness coach, project leader, or friend who may want to partner up with you for a shared Radical Reinvention. Simultaneously, evaluate if you have something to exchange. What do you have that can be beneficial to others? You may need all these people, and it's best to determine this now. It takes a village and never forget that. My mentors, male and female, and advisors, were instrumental to my career success. Don't ever underestimate the importance of male mentors and advisors. Men are not the enemy. They can get you where you want to be fast and become great friends as well. This is important to remember.

Resources take time to assemble, and relationships take time to grow. Each one of my treasured colleagues, who I spent a lot of time with on Zoom during the pandemic, know today that they can connect with me for anything. I want to help them define and reach their career goals. It was during this time that I reflected on all my mentors and what each has represented at different stages of my life.

Carrie Donovan, iconic editor at *Vogue, Harper's Bazaar*, and *The New York Times*, took me to *Bazaar* with her as senior fashion editor. She was vivacious and fun and always knew what she wanted and how to get it. Everyone loved her, big personality, funny and I loved her for carrying me through this exhilarating journey. She was also the Old Navy Lady in all their early commercials. She was a character with a great persona and sense of humor, as well as style.

Anna Wintour, who I had worked with at *Harper's Bazaar* and who has contributed to the fashion industry in front of and behind the scenes more than anyone could ever write about, is another woman I admire. Her name is on the wing of the Costume Institute at The Metropolitan Museum of Art. She is a force.

Fashion photographer, Billy Cunningham, whose vision was always so electrifying and now, elevated so many of my editorial assignments with his professional lens. I still look at his photographs to jar my own creativity. He knew the fashion 'street scene' better than anyone in the world.

Carine Roitfeld, former French *Vogue* editor-in-chief, is my fashion icon. I just love her look, her talent, and her spirit. She is another force to be reckoned with.

My mother, Marie Lippe, was one of the most important women and role models in my life. Again, she was a successful model and then a businesswoman in the fashion industry who was a great mother, grandmother, wife, friend, confidant, and a great cook. She had it all, especially courage and confidence. And she was beautiful inside and out. When my friends were in trouble or needed a shoulder to cry on, they went to my mom. She was the first person I hired at Lippe Taylor, and she stayed on for more than twelve years and lived with us in the city and went home on the weekends. That's saying a lot. She also had a terrific Irish sense of humor and had a major impact on my son and the character and humanity he exemplifies today. Generations living today in the home is a very special and often underappreciated value in this country.

My father, William Lippe, was a huge figure and very important man in my life. I idolized my dad. I was the only girl; we had a very close and loving relationship. Fortunately, we spent a lot of time together particularly after he retired from Seagram's where he oversaw marketing and sales, a position that was demanding and involved a lot of travel. Both my parents instilled in me a very strong work ethic.

My brothers, Billy and Michael, were my best pals and also advisors and fierce protectors. They were my 'rocks' in life. Always there for me, always ready to punch a date out and always ready to straighten me out when I was going down a wrong track. I was so fortunate to have such a close, loving, and protective family. Their love and protection gave me so much confidence even as a young girl. I talk to my brother, Michael, almost every day. He's been there for me in a very special way since my husband passed. I am who I am today because of each of them.

Never forget the significance of developing mentors at a young age and they can be family members. I have looked back on the steppingstones and opportunities these people created for me. Also, working for a brand name and highly respected company like *Vogue* so early on in my career was such a good way to get started in launching a career. I was able to use many of these relationships and their lessons which helped support the first amazing and defining assignments of my new communications agency. Simply priceless resources. I always strive to pass it forward and have mentored many younger women which is so rewarding for me. It's good karma and gives you great purpose. Many of these women are still in my life. I value each one of them, particularly my colleagues at Lippe Taylor who teach me every day and give me the strength to push forward. They are now my mentors, and I am the mentee. It's a beautiful thing how that happens.

Fool-Proof and Finance-Proof Your Reinvention

Liza Andrews teaches us how to identify when people are getting in the way and finding the right resources that will aid us. "During my years coaching clients and researching the psychology of change, I discovered that some of the strong reasons of our resistance is related to our social identity. When it comes to one of the most important types of reinvention—career—I noticed that what prevents most individuals from switching paths is not only the obvious financial aspects, but also, the fear of being misjudged by those whose opinions matter to them. I call these obstacles 'social filters'. They cause us to consider other people's perception of our reinvention, approving only those which seem logical and show evidence of future success. In practical terms, after applying such filters, my options are deflated from 'I can become anything I want' to 'I can do something new *within reason*.'

"This self-consciousness inhibits true reinvention based on the individual's passions and natural talents, creating instead, an opportunity for a 'partial reinvention' that allows some level of change for the individual, without threatening the *status quo*. After the pandemic, the whole world was shaken by the fear of dying younger than planned, and this gave many of us the push to dare leaving our jobs and even marriages in search of our true callings. I compared this information with data I had collected along several more-stable years, and still, to most career reinventions, some type of filter was applied during the decision-making process. Your chances of making radical changes will depend on how sensitive you are to social bullying and how determined you are to *rebranding* and letting the world know—and respect—your updated self."

I love this moniker, "updated self" for when we need a break from thinking of our reinvention as a radical one. It softens but does not take away from the task at hand. We update wardrobes, resumes, appliances, and operating systems all the time. Apple nudges me to update something every other day, jeez! Update yourself.

Andrews recommends the following steps:

1. Be logical when it comes to the finances, which will back up your new choices. Ideally, one should have at least one year of savings covering all their basic expenses, before leaving their jobs to start something new that will require a learning curve and perhaps making little or no money.

2. Move your desired career from the *hobby* to the *partial job* category. Reorganize your life to devote more time to the career you are considering and start establishing connections in the new field to

test the waters. Conciliate these efforts with your current job for a while, until you are in a safer place to make the move. This will give you a clear picture of what may be only a dream and test your convictions. The experience may surprise you by helping you realize that the desired career is not really for you and should continue to be simply a form of entertainment. Starting this engine will give you the enthusiasm to endure the rest of the necessary journey to get to your passion. Equally important, this step-by-step will serve as evidence to your support system that your reinvention, no matter how radical, has a plan, and you should be able to navigate this process without losing their respect.

3. Once you commit to going through with this gradual, sensible process, allow yourself the freedom to fully embrace your reinvention plan. You do want to have a support system if you fail. Be aware, however, that in some cases, your support system will be too rigid to accommodate a radical personal or career reinvention, even if perfectly orchestrated.

She adds: "Reinvention processes conducted within the limits of socially imposed filters are not reinventions; they are *adjustments* that won't make your life more meaningful, causing you to remain unfulfilled and often, depressed. That's the crucial point where you cannot allow collective apprehension or over-caution to keep you from exploring, searching for your best self and the life you dreamed of."

CRAIG STANLAND: FROM PRISONER TO REINVENTION ARCHITECT

AFTER HITTING ROCK bottom while in federal prison, Craig Stanland was forced to make a choice: give up or reinvent himself. He had it all—the nice house, expensive cars, watches, and fancy dinners—until his preoccupation with the materialism and status made him lose sight of what's truly important, and he made the worst decision of his life: defrauding one of the biggest tech companies in the world. His actions resulted in him losing everything, including his own self-worth.

Through the painful, terrifying process of starting over, Craig ultimately discovered that when you lose everything, anything is possible. Today, Craig is an author, speaker, and reinvention architect. He specializes in working with high achievers who've chased success, money, and status in the first half of their lives, only to find a success-sized hole in their lives. He helps them tap into their full potential, break free from autopilot, draft a new life blueprint, and connect with their life's calling so they can live their extraordinary second half with purpose, meaning and fulfillment.

Here, he discusses tips for breaking out of the prison we create for ourselves by living an inauthentic life.

When you think life is over, reinvent.

When I was sentenced to serve two years in a federal prison, life ended in my mind. I barely heard any of the words the judge spoke; all I saw was the end of my life.

The stress of the case and pending prison sentence made me lose a lot of weight. I was only 111 pounds when the judge sentenced me; I graduated high school weighing 118. I was forty-one years old and weighed less than when I graduated high school. I remember wearing these terrible shoes, which I hated, because my attorney told me it would be a "bad look" to go in wearing expensive shoes. I bought my terrible shoes from Target the day before and they were incredibly uncomfortable! The judge was going through all this legalese that I couldn't understand, I'm weak from the weight loss, I'm massively uncomfortable, and felt as though I had no idea what was happening.

I didn't know about the different prison security levels, so I literally thought I was going to get raped and beaten every day. Fortunately, this didn't happen, but other nightmares did. My crime and incarceration led to divorce, financial ruin, and stripped me of my identity. And all this led to dark thoughts, including those of suicide.

I loved writing and creating as a child, but slowly my creativity died with the responsibilities of adulthood. When I began having thoughts of suicide in prison, I was terrified to share that with anybody, because in prison, if you tell someone you are suicidal or share it with family over the phone or friends in prison, they lock you in solitary confinement. That scared the hell out of me, so pen and paper became my outlet to process my thoughts of wanting to die. A friend reminded me of my love of writing. I had written a driver's ed video script in high school and a draft of our senior play. I remember thinking, *that wasn't that long ago.* To have him remind me of that passion and creativity fueled me to continue writing and that is when it started to dawn on me, writing is cathartic and transformative.

One thing you have a lot of in prison is time. In Otisville Federal Prison, we had about 7,500 books in the library and most federal inmates can receive paperbacks from Amazon. The library became my outlet. I read and wrote every day.

Radical Reinvention is not supposed to be easy; never give up.

It took me six years to write my book, *Blank Canvas: How I Reinvented My Life After Prison* and publish it. If you have ever read *American Gods* by Neil Gaiman, you'll be familiar with the protagonist, Shadow. He's a mountain of a man, strong, big, and silent. He dies and is forced to stand in front of the gods naked and alone and meant to face every single shameful moment of his entire life. He had to relive every terrible thing. When I opened the box of the first fifty hardcopies of my book, that is how I felt, naked in front of the gods. I cried. My tears were immediately followed by elation, purpose, and joy. It had been torturous to write; the power of putting everything, the good, the bad, the painful and the ugly, out there.

I recently spoke at my aunt's book club. I have shared the stage with FBI agents, secret service, but this felt more intimidating because of the collective wisdom in the room. Toward the end of the presentation, one of the members spoke. She had just lost her husband and suffered a stroke, but she said through a cascade of tears, "Your book has shown me that I have a second chance. It gave me hope."

Her words reminded me of the purpose of writing my book—to give people hope that they can find meaning again after tragedy or simply after having pursued what they thought would make them happy and realizing that it does not.

Identify how you want to feel in your life, activities to do.

I have rebuilt my life from the ground up, and it took a great deal of conscious effort.

I have what I call an "inner foundation" among a series of building terms as a reinvention architect. There is an underlying theme among all those who come to me: Life isn't what they thought it would be and they want it to be different. What we do is establish that clarity on what it is that they want in their life. It's very rarely materialistic.

What my clients are looking for is more peace; more freedom; more creativity; more connection; more meaning. I
help my clients tap into those emotions, then help them
identify the activities that produce those emotions. I help
them cultivate their own inner foundation.

Unwind old beliefs or needs holding you back.

I was recently on a discovery call with a potential client.
This person has a good job, making good money, but he
was missing that meaning and fulfillment in his life. I said,
"What do you like to do? What makes you feel good?"
He told me he liked to work with his hands, especially
woodworking. I asked him why he didn't do it if he knew
it would make him happy. His response: "Well, I don't
want to sell what I make. I don't want it to be this big,
giant business." We began to explore this, and he realized
that he had this limiting belief from his parents that every
single thing he does has to generate revenue.

We were able to process and heal that belief, and he
started woodworking. He sends me pictures of the bar he
made for his house, stools, tables, and now he is making
things for friends. This hobby brings him joy, meaning,
and fulfillment, and has connected him with the inner
courage to land him an even better job that gives him a
deeper sense of fulfillment as well.

The key is to get clear on what you want, the obstacle you perceive is in your way, and then to give yourself
permission to do the thing that will lead to meaning, connection and peace in your life.

We can have a deep intellectual understanding of

something; for example, the dangers of smoking. We can want to quit smoking, but that cigarette gives us something. It serves something. When we understand what that cigarette means to us, we can begin to understand the meaning we are attributing to it and undo those beliefs.

Reinvention is the path to meaning, purpose and fulfillment.

You're never too old to reinvent. You do not have to burn it all to the ground to start over. I had to face these myths just like I now help my clients to do. "I'm fifty-two, I can't reinvent." "I'm sixty. Who am I to reinvent?" "I'm a CFO, I can't become an author without completely divorcing myself from that identity and that job." Work through all those myths and understand in the silliest terms, you can walk and chew gum at the same time! Use the skills you already possess to make incremental steps. Making small steps everyday toward your goals will be radically rewarding.

Reflection on Craig's Radical Reinvention

Craig is a real person who made mistakes, paid the price, and returned to the most prized parts of himself to write a new life. Most of us will not serve time in prison with so much time on our hands to bounce our reflections off the walls. Craig's true gift of helping others reinvent would not have come to the surface if he didn't choose *life*. At the same time, I can attest to the notion that every day can be rewarding as you work through reinvention. The first stage, Review, is always the hardest. But now your life is a *Blank Canvas*, as Craig's book title reminds us.

CHAPTER 8

REBRAND

"Brand is not a product, that's for sure; it's not one item. It's an idea, it's a theory, it's a meaning, it's how you carry yourself. It's aspirational, it's inspirational."

—*KEVIN PLANK,*
BUSINESSMAN

Stage 8 of Your Radical Reinvention—REBRAND

Resolution and Recommendations for:

Leadership | Followership | Messaging
| Culture | Marketing | Sales

I'VE BEEN REINVENTING brands for over thirty years. With all this vast experience, I've learned that so much wisdom transfers from the personal brand to rich, renowned corporate brands, which then is reinforced through representation—presence, leadership, empathy, communications, culture. There are common denominators in all branding. But I am not trying to be tricky or even strategic by reserving so much savory content for this "branding" section as a grand finale.

Our Radical Re-Inventors are powerful brands. You are a brand. I am my own brand of many reinventions, starting as a tough New York City kid moving to the suburbs of New Jersey and then returning to the big city first chance I got. And I'm still there. That's who I am: a New York City girl. That wasn't easy for a young girl to navigate going from the city to the suburbs. Then, as the amusing junior in high school who knew nobody. Transferring schools and entertaining the most popular girl in the eleventh grade was my first reinvention milestone. This was also when I realized that I had to "sell" myself to her and her peers to survive—and perhaps even thrive—for the next two years of high school.

It cannot be understated that everyone must learn how to sell themselves, even when they're just teenagers. Whether you deliberately hone sales skills or not, you are always selling. Call it whatever you want but know it's sales. Life is selling in one form or another if you want to be successful. My collaborator on this book sold me on herself within a few minutes of meeting. She came after me by phone, I liked her spirit, her Southern accent, we had a meeting, she sold me on herself in one hour and that was that. Matches for the great opportunities possible in this life are instinctual. Women have great instinctual gifts, but we have to use them and trust them. They don't necessarily require an address book of accolades to build trust or show capability. We mimic those we're selling to. At Lippe Taylor, public relations and almost everything we do incorporates selling, whether it's creating and selling in big ideas, pitching media/influencers on a new drug or presenting new business plans to clients all day long with skill, strategy, creative and the data to support all our brilliant insights. It's a science and it's an art. Always be mindful that you are always selling your personal brand and frequently—even when you least expect it. If you feel more comfortable with phrases like "making a great impression", "influencing", "resonating", own it, but always be aware there is a buyer, or numerous buyers, in your peripheral checking you out and your personal brand.

Irina Soriano, vice president of a technology company and a pioneer in her professional field, advocates for the next generation, Generation Brand, those born between 2012 and 2030. She wrote a modern playbook for cultivating what she calls our "life-brand". Our life-brand, aka our digital fingerprint, significantly impacts our personal and professional lives. She explains, "Wherever you work, your life-brand becomes part of the company brand. Whatever employees do on their (semi-) private or public social channels also represents their employer. Everything is unified. Any like, love, post, or comment lives in the cloud forever and can be discovered even years later. We have a responsibility to actively control our life-brand considering the vast impact things we share on social media can have on our communities and the companies we work for. But life-brand goes beyond what we say and do on social media. Especially for Generation Brand, what is done and said when pictures and videos are taken can significantly change or diminish one's future career and professional path. Unpublished photos and videos are as much part of our life-brand, even if they have not been published yet."

Irina emphasizes building your life-brand around your identity and purpose. "The concept of life-brand goes beyond the concept of personal branding and brings different components together. It identifies one person as distinct from others and is defined by the person's unique purpose and identity through their everyday displayed public behavior and chosen language in the real and virtual world, shaping the public's perception about the life-brand owner. Your purpose will likely change over the course of your life. My purpose evolved and shaped for years. It started centered on my professional life and has then expanded. Controlling one's life-brand from an early age is critical especially for Generation Brand with cancel culture having already impacted many teenagers and young adults. Social media education and guardrails are key."

I wanted Irina to thread her own life-brand together to teach this seamless program for *Radical Reinvention*. Think of every lesson in this book as a tool. The power and implications of life-brand speak to nearly all facets of radical reinvention. It's not just about presentation or representation to the outside world as "image". We present what we feel and know. The tone and tenor of that solo work—review, recovery, reawakening, remembering who we are, reimagining, reaching—shows up in the unveiling, our life-brand.

From a deeply personal lens on life-brand, she shares, "Sometimes reinvention comes from challenges we encounter in life. My personal life-brand has gone through many changes since I started to actively control it. From a significant career change to a minor health crisis, my life-brand has grown and evolved. These challenges have made it stronger over the years."

Irina models Radical Reinvention. She didn't plan it, but she was aware of her life-brand and impact before disruption. She handled the disruption and became a better leader. She is an authentic, empathetic leader. I hear no compromise of brand. She strengthened it and updated it, serving herself, her family, her company, and everyone she touches.

Lead Like There's No Tomorrow

In addition to the creepy virus ball we saw branded in all Pantone colors during the pandemic, did you encounter a vampire? Be honest! Okay, I'm not talking about the shamelessly hot ones in "Twilight" or "Diaries". I'm speaking of the 'bloodsucking leaders' walking this earth with toxic tendencies to spread fear, foreboding, and damnation inside their own version of the Dark Ages business-style. Beware of what I call "bleedership". No one follows cruel, know-it-all managers or bosses with no humanity or humility. Today, young people are losing hope in the future and the older generation feels something important is lost. There is a serious epidemic of loneliness according to the US surgeon general, presenting a profound public health threat compared to smoking and obesity creating a greater risk of depression, anxiety and even heart disease, stroke, and dementia. The aim is to rally Americans to spend more time together as family, friends and in the workplace too with colleagues.

As reported in *Forbes*, the pressure the pandemic put on employees and employers who struggled to produce under difficult circumstances, caused workers to realize they no longer had to accept outdated methods of work and a transactional relationship with an employer that treats them as means of growth and production rather than as humans. The "command-and-control approach" is outdated and hardly respected. Progressive leaders now must treat employees as stakeholders and build relationships with team members based on acknowledging and fulfilling their need for adequate compensation and benefits, autonomy, flexibility, development, and wellbeing in both the workplace and in their personal lives, resulting in increased commitment, productivity, and retention. Authenticity and even vulnerability goes a long way. Avoidance might feel good in the moment, but it is without courage. Courage is being familiar with failure, disappointment and even heartbreak. Inspiration and imagination are imperative. The softer side of leadership is deeply valued today with more empathetic, compassionate, transparent attributes, but always with strict accountability, so everyone knows where they stand and what's expected of them. Being optimistic with creativity and imagination is a plus. And humor goes a long way, too.

You have to show your team that they matter. Share your voice and ideas, your wisdom, but allow them to give an opinion anytime, even contrary to yours. Listening is an imperative skill today. This *is* inclusion. Leadership today is about shaping culture, connecting people, and creating an environment where humanity is respected and expected. It's a high-touch, as well as high-tech, environment where people must come first. Values cannot be challenged. The more you are grounded in your values, your humanity, the better chance you will succeed. Lead with intention.

Lippe Taylor employees are expected to trust and respect their colleagues. We can tell within three weeks if someone is right for our company or not—if you come in and start making demands, raise your voice, humiliate a colleague, you're gone, you cannot succeed. We will not and cannot tolerate behavior like this. Our staff won't accept it. It's just not our shared mission nor can it be part of our culture.

The whole humanity of how you live your life—how you treat your teams, family, your doorman, Uber driver—doing it all with more humanity is vital. Kindness and respect go a long way today. The pandemic has brought it to the surface. People are thinking more about this now. Empathy is essential. You stand out now when you're not empathetic. Leadership with empathy, intelligence, and humanity balances concern about staff mental wellness, in addition to productivity and strict accountability. Many leaders did not think in these terms, pre-pandemic, but they must return to their human side and reinvent their approach right now to succeed in this new world order. Forgive people and move on. Be your imperfectly perfect self. Show up. Lead from your heart, not your hurt.

What does team culture look like? How are you as a leader in this shifting time? This all speaks to reinvention. It's the emotional side and the caring side of leadership.

Without that, people won't follow you. Self-awareness is critical; keep your promises and let other people make decisions. The people business is not only about colleagues. The harder calls are with clients. If we take a client by mistake, those who scream and make our people feel less valued, we must remove ourselves from those toxic relationships.

People say, "I never get the Sunday night blues at Lippe Taylor." That is a great compliment. Most people that work with us tell us their feelings about the company. We try to keep an open dialogue and do frequent surveys. We have a thoughtful interview process. "She/he is so Lippe Taylor." I've learned the hard way that you must correct mistakes very quickly because it permeates the brand. Culture is key; you have to work hard to keep the happiness, gratitude, kindness, courage, optimism, purpose, joy, love, belonging, inclusivity, equity, diversity, strict accountability and the great work, so people always know what's expected of them and where they stand. Cheer for them when they've done something special. You also have to navigate as a trusted team how to have difficult conversations with each other. You must be able to forgive people and move on.

We can move on if we lose a client, but what is the key learning? We carefully review the mistakes we all made and try not to make the same ones again. I don't tear my hair out and make everyone feel less of a professional. We were all in it together and we all failed together. We discuss the failure; dissect where and how we went wrong. A tenant of the brand is inquiry and curiosity. Asking sincere questions to get to the heart of the matter. Have you thought about that? This? It's rational because the decision is frequently irrational. I remember every client firing and every new piece of business we didn't get. However, a bad client giving heart palpations to valued staff gets in the way of your entire culture. Sometimes it's so much money or such a designer brand and it's hard to let go, but we do. We have to. It's easier to find a new client than replace the extraordinary people working on the account. We're living in a data-centric world, but it doesn't override our loyalty to our people. We are people first, and we're not just saying that to make you like us.

Everyone needs to look inside. They must be purpose-driven now if they weren't before. The purpose/ mission, if tightly woven inside, can thwart these emotions that do not add to your reinvention game.

Nick Taylor adds: "Have you been around people who've read too many self-help books? Their interaction is based on things they've read. You're like, *no way*. That's not Lippe Taylor leadership. Our whole business has been the people business, without feeling contrived, due to my mother's leadership style and the culture she established of bringing a communal element of listening, caring, close engagement, personal touch—and delivering outstanding results for our clients."

I, too, must return to my signature personal skills Nick noted, what makes me ME, from time to time. There was no greater test for this than facing devices and screens every day and activating Zoom with little personal connection. After all, we're a creative agency known for big innovation, strategic creative and intelligent people who execute big ideas that grow our clients' business, supported by splashy, strategic events for full immersion with our client base and their consumers. Big, bold, and smart is a major part of our brand. In order to keep winning, we had to reset. We had to transfer our energy to screens and one-hundred-plus-page proposals delivered online. We no longer could depend on the personal touch. To know us, to feel us in a room is to love us, trust us, hire us. That didn't work so well on Zoom. Yet, we doubled our business during the pandemic. Go figure.

We must learn to always be ready for change. Nick suggests, "Expand your mind! I've seen people in the marketing industry be very attached to old ideals and therefore, very difficult and stubborn to get them to accept change. I've seen the resistance like, 'oh, you young Millennials with your Twitter, TikTok, Instagram' and now ChatGPT. In the context of any industry, just going with change and surrendering yourself to change is important. Being on top of it and understanding it and reading modern and smart business publications for trends in your industry is so important. Be in touch. Be curious. Understand culture. Get on the platform and experience how TikTok works. See why everyone is on Instagram and how it works. And be sure to learn all about AI and how it's going to change the world as we know it. Develop your attention span. Read marketing and leadership books. Stay curious and connected. Podcasts are a great way to stay informed. There are new technologies in terms of human development that more people should be aware of. Microdosing will be more in the mainstream particularly when today, loneliness, anxiety and depression are the leading conditions. It's real, it's here and it might be beneficial.

It's the new consciousness evolution. Read about it. Know about it."

Dr. Zhexembayeva, who has helped thousands of leaders reinvent, strongly urges that a few things are required today and if we don't do them, we are dooming our companies. "One is to stop thinking of change as a rare event. It is a norm of daily life. Second, start actively and very aggressively helping your team enjoy change in whichever way you can pair change with joy, this will save you so much headache. It will reduce resistance to change. It will accelerate the speed. It will create so much resource for the ingenuity required for the renewal process. We cannot be creative and imaginative in a state of stress. It's biologically impossible because the way stress response works, we literally do not have enough supply of blood to our brain. This is not personal choice. We literally don't have enough oxygen brought to our brain by blood to be creative, so unless your teams actually have fun, enjoy, laugh, feel heard, associate change with something that you all look forward to, they will not be able to invent the mass amount of small, incremental and radical changes they need to bring about every day change in our world of constant uncertainty, constant disruption, constant volatility. Be as aggressive as you can in this task of pairing reinvention with joy."

LVMH: Preserving Heritage While Elevating Experiences

The SVP of Strategic Enterprise Capabilities at Moët Hennessy USA, Carlos Zepeda epitomizes life-brand. Hailing from Mexico, he wrangled reinvention initiatives for ten years at PepsiCo, then Havaianas USA, opening stores in New York City's Oculus and Miami. As he tells it, "I went from being in a $70 billion company to a $1 billion company. That was a transition. In the end, it showed me that I could learn and adapt again and reinvent myself. Brazilians and Americans are a different corporate culture. It doesn't get more American than Pepsi. It doesn't get more Brazilian than Havaianas."

When Zepeda took his reinvention skills to the houses of Belvedere within LVMH, he was at home. The company is renowned for having a reinvention culture and reinterpreting its products through entrepreneurial spirit, cross-functional exposure, and international experience. Some of the brands have been established for hundreds of years. So, how do you preserve heritage of storied brands, honoring the craft and the people who created yet reinvent for the culture of now…without messing up their DNA? Louis Vuitton paved the way by inserting hip hop street culture as luxury in newer looks.

Zepeda explains, "It's an entrepreneurial-family business. What do you need? Do it. Let's create. While respecting and being the guardians of the brands. In some cases, century-old ones. It's part of the fabric of the company, and you are always surrounded by inspiration between the brands you represent, or a colleague represents. You're all part of the group. The experience you have abroad like visiting a champagne Maison, where they give you the history, the *crayères* of Veuve and you see signs of when it was a hospital in the war. Madame Cliquot's story as a female creator and entrepreneur. The culture is very lively and stimulating intellectually and emotionally. You're always *feeling* things. It's a fertile environment to create. There is creative tension between the brand homes and the markets."

What is key to rebranding? Is there a tasty formula that only LVHM is privy to? According to Zepeda:

- Curiosity and courage
- Aspiration and inspiration
- Transparency and vulnerability
- Sensations and emotions
- Embedding strategy into the process, as familiarity drives adoption
- Even a bad idea is progress because you know that's not "the one". Having an idea is already a win. Growth mindset is imperative.

He adds, "This is empirical from what I've seen, but by nature, people do not like change. People are motivated differently, and if you acknowledge that motivation, they will be more open to change. Don't be a one-trick pony just regurgitating steps. It's psychology and mindset. Change is hard, but it can be exciting. Having shared goals and connecting people to broader thinking impacts them and works well. Vulnerability should be a common place for exploration. I want to take more risks and push even further to grow myself and have more impact. Having an ever-evolving vision of yourself, career plan, your life, you can maximize what you can do. If you only have one version of what you want to be, that's hard because outside forces penetrate the walls! Don't be afraid of becoming somebody you haven't been."

I need to stop and swoon over that last line because it's worth imagining the emotions and sensations associated with the possibility of becoming someone you have never been before. Personally, I'm thinking Bond Girl–fierce, fearless, smart, confident, self-aware, and always vulnerable. As Craig Stanland inquired, how do you want to feel in your life?

"Early in my career, I once received feedback that I didn't know how to talk to executives," shares Zepeda. He had to review this disruption. "Being real, I didn't know what to do with it. I was on Metro North coming back home thinking, what a bummer. Then I started to analyze myself. I followed up with my manager for more. Did I not have executive presence? Was I not assertive? She gave me more input. What I realized is that I had grown up in a different culture where you are not always grabbing the mic, speaking up. The other part was lack of confidence. That awareness taught me to be more vocal and more courageous and speaking up and seeing what would happen. It was a defining moment. Now, I am driving transformation of a multinational company for the CEO. I'm a cancer survivor. I had cancer when I was six years old. I was at MD Anderson for a couple years and one of the first kids that doctors practiced chemotherapy on. Because of what I experienced, I have an internal thirst for life. I saw that it could expire at a young age. It's part of me. I have the reinvention gene, an energy I apply to every second of my life."

What did the LVMH story, many brand houses, many stories, evoke? What about Carlos Zepeda? I hope your inner chatter is all about branding. I told you I would go under the knife. This includes revealing more about the brand I started thirty years ago. Lippe Taylor recently celebrated its thirtieth anniversary with an epic party in New York City with our amazing staff, clients, and friends. It was our very emotional, sensational reward for our very Radical Reinvention.

Lippe Taylor's Radical Rebranding: Exalted for a New Era

There are very few industries, if any, that have been upended and reinvented as much as media. From the late 80s to the early 2020s, the height of the media industry was being totally decimated by Google, Facebook, Netflix, Spotify. And now, ChatGPT is changing and challenging everything. As Lippe Taylor strives to be among the best at inserting brands into culture through earned media, creative and social media, it's our business to be ahead of the trend at every step.

We have over 100 clients today. Botox, Nestle, Citi, Pfizer, Keurig Dr. Pepper, to just name a few. What does it take to win these storied clients? A lot of hard work. A lot of grit. Research. Leadership. Leading the team consistently to put in the same amount of work. A strategic, creative business plan that we present to a client to win their business can be over one hundred pages. Smart data, insightful insights, and great creative to inspire and excite them and see their own business in a different way is imperative. Sometimes, it takes the heart and soul out of you because it's very difficult to understand a brand when you just receive a short brief, and you have ten days to develop their communications plan. We comb through their materials, conduct proprietary research and analytics. We come in with data that they have never seen. The data and analytics are our secret sauce. Our creative is always very strong, but others come with this, too. These ideas used to be based a lot on intuition and research the agency would do and feel. Six, seven years ago, it became so apparent to me that if I didn't have the data/analytics that supported the insight that drove the strategy, we weren't going to win any more on creative alone. And then there is the presentation to the client, which is extremely important. I had to reinvent Lippe Taylor to meet this new shift and fast to meet the new demand.

Brendan Kane talks about shaking the rust out of your brain. I concur! In his book, *Hook Point: How to Stand Out in a 3-Second World*, he asserts, "A lot of people know who they are, what they do, and a few even know why they do it—but even when brands or individuals have clarity in these areas, they often struggle to grab a potential audience's attention for long enough to get them to learn about their attributes. Others have amazing products or services that fail to achieve great success because they don't know how to talk about what they do effectively. This is because digital and social media have reshaped our world into one of micro-attention.

"There are over sixty billion messages shared on digital platforms each day, and the average person is exposed to thousands of ads a day. This bombardment of stimuli has changed the way we communicate and market content both online and off. In fact, research shows that you have less than three seconds to capture a person's attention.

With such a short window of time, we need to hook audiences quickly, efficiently, and consistently if we want to successfully fuel brand awareness and growth." This quick, efficient approach no longer had room for showcasing my passion and intuition.

In 2015, I lost business because the company was not digital enough, and we didn't have the data. I hired every digital superstar in New York City. They were the smartest people in the room, but they couldn't manage others. They were brilliant at explaining what "should" be done, but never able to actually do it. Honestly, after cycling through many consultants, I knew our days were numbered if we didn't bring in a transformational leader who was capable of changing the agency and seriously bringing us into the Digital Age. I didn't want my agency to become a dinosaur. I knew I was forward thinking, having started many successful programs for many big companies. I had to figure this out and quickly.

I was not looking for a president, but someone I respected and who knew the agency business, called, and beamed, "You need to meet this guy!" He wants to run a company, and I think he had hoped I would let him run mine. At the same time, many offers were coming in to purchase the company, my baby that I had conceived and built up in a reinvention of my own. I would not just hand it over to any person or entity. When I did, it was an easy transition because that force of nature was Paul Dyer.

Paul is a master at analytics and data, digital and everything else needed in a leader to run a successful agency today. Within four months, I knew that this guy knew what he was doing. He came from a big agency. Great thinker, great writer, strong leader. His former agency didn't have the empathy or humanity that was the cornerstone of Lippe Taylor. In the beginning, he was flabbergasted at why things seemed to take so long. Why did people spend so much time "inefficiently" talking things through? Why did they bring so much of their personal lives into work? His previous agency had been massively successful, he thought, because they were so focused on the bottom line. Every meeting was rushed. Every conversation focused on business. People were there to work, not chitchat! Quickly, Paul realized his previous company had been successful despite those things, not because of them. Lippe Taylor had stood the test of time because of our culture, as well as the great work. And our culture revolved around people understanding and supporting one another. Sometimes that meant spending more time in a meeting to ensure we had alignment. On the back end, that meant the work would be executed flawlessly, though, and every person on the team would feel valued and respected in the process, leading to higher retention of our people and our clients.

To his credit, Paul recognized this quickly. He became a strong leader and we worked seamlessly together. He was also very thoughtful in identifying the areas where I excelled, ensuring the value I brought was still being felt throughout the agency and the work. Together, we learned to complement each other perfectly. He changed the whole dynamic of the agency, and it was a thrilling time for me.

Importantly, after you have founded a company in your apartment with your baby crawling on the floor, knowing when to say you don't have the goods to take your company through the next five years, is vulnerable and valuable. Areas of my business changed so dramatically with social, digital, influencer and now AI, our new proposition needed to capitalize on the great creative we were lauded for, with good data, to put us in a position of leadership. We had always been exceptionally creative. That's why we won almost every piece of business we competed for. Also, we had the best and brightest teams. It was easier when we were smaller to be extra creative. When you're larger, you're spreading your creatives thin. We invested in the best big-idea creatives to lead the way in our reinvention.

Paul and I reimagined the company. I needed new data, analytics, and great research. I could no longer go in and win business based on intuition and my own creative mind. *Screw your intuition! Where's your data?* Paul describes this era in the words of Jim Barksdale, former CEO of Netscape, who famously said, "If we have data, let's look at data. If all we have are opinions, let's go with mine." Clients were no longer interested in my opinion only, regardless of how much experience backed it up. Without the data, they would simply go with their own gut.

Paul and I were put together for a reason and the stars were aligned. Being introduced to Paul was one of the most important things that's happened to me in my business. We were meant to be together for reasons we didn't even understand at the time. He came in and together, we reimagined, and we doubled the business through COVID-19. During this time, he also wrote the classic, insightful book, *Friction Fatigue: What the Failure of Advertising Means for Future-Focused Brands.* Within weeks, it was on the business bestseller lists.

From my perspective, one hire made a huge difference. Paul is quick to remind me there were many others who we hired together that created the change we needed, which I'm well-aware of. But without him, none of it would have happened. Together, we redefined the agency. We decided where to invest and then invested in more super smart people. Paul interviews everybody. I have good instincts about people. You know your gut will usually serve you well, but it doesn't always. You make mistakes.

The company was morphed into something entirely different. Not the culture, however. I fought hard to keep it intact with all the growth we were experiencing. At the Christmas party last year, I must have had fifteen or twenty new people tell me they never knew a company like this existed. That it's possible to do what they do with such kind, smart people. They didn't think a culture like ours could prevail in a successful agency. It's hard to keep it; it's easy to mess it up, plain and simple. Everyone in the company must know and agree to the values and respect them. Sometimes you can toughen up a culture as long as it's done with trust and respect, and everyone is invested.

I always worked with women. *Vogue*, all women, *Bazaar*, women. Lippe Taylor, women. And I've trained so many young women who would start at Lippe Taylor and carry on values that were specific to women in the workplace. We're courageous together. We win this business; we lose this business together. Some of them have been alongside me fifteen or twenty years, and they are still thriving and bringing great value and growth to the company.

Paul had to reinvent himself to come to Lippe Taylor and be successful. Prior to Lippe Taylor, he came from a very patriarchal company. He reported to the CEO, a man, who had nine of his ten direct reports that were men. With the exception of one very strong woman, all the other women in that company, regardless of their title, reported to a man. Serious decisions were made in cigar bars at 2:00 a.m. and decisions to fire people were made after hours of drinking. It's no wonder there weren't a lot of women in top positions there. He came to Lippe Taylor shortly after his first daughter was born and described the family-first culture as a big reason why. That doesn't mean it wasn't a big adjustment.

Lippe Taylor truly is family-first. Meaning, more than half of our leaders are going home every night to kids. They're not going to cigar bars. Lippe Taylor is also woman-founded and women-powered. Meaning, a lot happens in conversation, a lot of dialogue takes place instead of just rushing to decisions. Before Lippe Taylor, Paul would talk to his CEO every couple of weeks. Usually, it was about revenue growth and new business wins. When he started at Lippe Taylor, I expected to talk with him every day—at length!

He reflects fondly, I think, on that time saying, "Maureen and I wouldn't just talk every day. We would talk for HOURS every day. It was about every little aspect of the business, the people, the clients, the work. Then at the end of the week, she would come into my office and say, 'You know, I feel like we didn't get any time together this week.' I couldn't believe it! How was I ever going to get anything done?! Of course, what I came to understand is that the investment of time in really understanding one another and the business led to much stronger alignment and much better execution later. In my previous company, fifteen-minute meetings would culminate with a list of action items, then everyone would sprint to the next thing. Nobody understood or trusted one another. Everybody had a slightly different understanding of the action items. And the incentives were to willfully misinterpret the meeting in favor of your own best interests. At Lippe Taylor, that simply didn't happen."

I asked Paul to share some examples that bring his own experience of reinventing in order to lead Lippe Taylor. In his words, he shares the story of his first day on the job.

"I was supposed to start in the middle of January. But the agency had a big new business pitch come in. I had already left my other job and had a brief vacation. Maureen called me saying I needed to start early to help with this pitch. That Monday, I showed up for work, and the entire office looks empty. Maureen had put everyone in the big conference room, where unbeknownst to me she told them, 'I have hired a new president. Moving forward you will all report to him, and he will report to me... and, here he is!' She opens the door and in I walk having no idea what's just transpired. So here I am, standing in front of a company with about sixty women and a few men scattered around. All of them are now staring at me like I must have come from planet Mars. It was a culture shock to say the least—for all of us. Thankfully, we made it through."

There are four reasons why we believe our transition was successful: Paul's approach, my approach, the support of a trusted lieutenant, and the strength of the company's culture. With Paul's own approach, he was firm and clear. But more importantly, he was also patient and curious about what made everyone tick. Paul put the time in to meet and understand each person.

Second was my unwavering support. Inevitably, situations would arise where people would come to me and complain about a decision Paul had made. I never wavered, and I never implied any dissent. If Paul had made a decision, that decision stood. If I actually disagreed with it, the person never realized it. Later, I would just approach Paul in private and we would talk about it.

Third was the impact of Lori Rubinson, the lieutenant. In an all-company meeting recently, Paul talked about the importance of Lori being what he calls the 'first follower' for him. Lori had everyone else's trust already, and she put the time in to get to know him. She saw that we were moving in the right direction, even if Paul didn't always handle things perfectly. She did an amazing job of assuring everyone this would be in the best interests of the company and their careers.

Fourth, the culture of Lippe Taylor was such that people were much less threatened by this new direction than you might expect.

Paul adds, "Here I was, a man with a left-brain, digital and analytics background, standing in front of a company full of women with right-brain creative and publicity careers, and telling them not to worry—they would be included, valued, and respected in this new era for the company. Meanwhile, I was hiring data scientists and technologists, introducing new financial and operational rigor, reorganizing teams so that some of the most fun parts of the job like coming up with creative ideas, were taken away and specialized in a group of new hires. All these things could very easily have scared people away. But the culture held strong. When I said they were important to our future, people believed me. They believed the company and Maureen had their best interests at heart."

It's worth it now to talk in more specifics about the Radical Reinvention of Lippe Taylor. As a traditional PR firm, Lippe Taylor was extraordinarily well-established as a firm that generated stellar media results with a particular focus on marketing to women. Because it was so well-established, it had a clear advantage in a certain corner of the industry. We had a lot of beauty, health, wellness, and fashion clients as a natural fit. However, this strong association also got in the way as we started to evolve the company. Clients, prospective employees, and the industry at large thought of us in a very narrow way. Paul and I talked about the enormous talent we had within the company. Our people had perfected skills that could be translated well beyond the scope of their current work. Therefore, it wasn't about replacing our people. We had to change what the outside world thought about us.

"One important aspect to how we changed perception is that we never tried telling people we were something different," says Paul. "It wasn't that we were suddenly going to stop being one thing and start being something else. We were still going to be a really good PR firm that excelled in marketing to women. And we were going to be much more than that, also."

This is a significant distinction, particularly given the context in the industry at that time. If you could rewind to the mid-2010s and look at every agency website, you would find there weren't any PR firms left. Technically, there were hundreds of course, but in that period of digital transformation and integrated, omnichannel marketing, public relations had become a bit of a dirty word. Even Edelman, the world's largest public relations firm, went through a period where it essentially disavowed the PR moniker. I never thought that was necessary or prudent for Lippe Taylor. For one thing, we really were *excellent* at public relations. And our clients and employees appreciated that. It was important to me that Paul believed it, also. He came from the digital world and had been responsible for one of the most successful digital transformation stories in our industry. For me to say PR was still important didn't carry much weight. For *him* to say it was a whole different thing.

"In 2016, I saw the pendulum swinging back," he explains. "We had the Presidential election, which brought with it the Cambridge Analytica scandal that forced programmatic media buying into an inglorious spotlight. On top of that, due to the election, everyone's social media feeds and search results were filled with... not ads. Not posts from friends. But news articles. News had become the centerpiece of the digital experience, and ironically, none of the PR firms wanted to be categorized that way anymore. I realized we could be true to our heritage while also becoming a digital powerhouse."

Here, you see the influence of the overall thought process and how comprehensive it was. We were maintaining internal culture, which would enable us to build new capabilities without fear that our existing talent or business would walk out the door. We had a narrative that was authentic about our reinvention. Still, would we be able to convince existing clients we had sufficiently reinvented? Or would their perceptions of the agency keep us in a box? Delicate nuances. Expensive ones, too! Our success here was largely thanks to the alignment between Paul and I from the start. He explains....

"At some point in the middle of 2016, Maureen and I sat down together for our first formal interview. I think it lasted two hours, and I met both her husband, Jerry, and her son, Nick. All of this, of course, presaged what the Lippe Taylor experience would truly be like. In that first conversation, though, Maureen told me that she needed someone who could bring in data and analytics capabilities and drive digital transformation of the company. I told her that's what I did, and in fact, it was my exact area of impact for both agencies I'd worked at previously. Then I asked her a crucial question. 'There are two ways you can go about digital transformation for a PR firm,' I said. 'There's the fast and painful way. Or the slow and expensive way. I want to know which path you're willing to take.' Of course, Maureen shifted uncomfortably and asked me to further explain. 'The fast and painful way is the path we took at my previous agency,' I said. 'I joined in March 2009 and within ninety days, we had over $1M of digital and social media work. The CEO decided this was the future, so he hired a big-time digital leader as my boss, and he told the whole company to either get on board the train or get run over by it. We lost dozens of great people over the next couple of years because they felt disrespected or cast aside. The culture of the company was gutted, and our north star was different depending on who you talked to. Honestly, the culture never really recovered from it. However, we were Digital Agency of the Year three of the next five years.' By this point Maureen was stone-faced as she stared at me, probably waiting for the next shoe to drop. I continued, 'We can do that. I have a giant network of these people because my last agency was a turnover machine. So, I can bring them all here, and we will be Digital Agency of the Year practically overnight...'

'Or we can take the second path, the slow and expensive way. In this path, I will hire people with a different sensibility. Those who want to collaborate with and bring your existing people along. But it won't happen overnight. Your existing people need to work alongside them for a year probably. Then, it's a process of winning more digital-first work, delivering the work with excellence, proving we can take on more, and so on. All the while, you're essentially paying for two salaries to do one-and-a-half jobs, because your existing people's digital skills aren't good enough yet, but the new hires aren't able to do the pre-existing work, either. Which means, we will maintain the culture and bring people along, but you need to agree to basically take a year with no profit.' To her credit, Maureen's entire body language changed. Where she had been leaning back, stone-faced while I described ripping apart the culture and creating a digital powerhouse overnight, now she became animated and leaned in, saying '*That* one. No doubt in my mind. I'm not doing this for me,' she said. 'I'm doing it because I've got a big group of people who I care deeply for. They have been incredibly loyal and are excellent at what they know how to do, but they don't know how to do the things you're talking about. It's my responsibility to bring them along and teach them; they have a whole career ahead of them. If they don't learn these skills, they are going to get left behind. Unfortunately, I can't give it to them. I've taught them what I know. If I don't figure it out soon, I will have done them a huge disservice.'

"Every time I tell this story, the hair on my neck tingles. It was one of those moments that freezes in time. Maureen talks about how she knew the importance of digital and data transformation from a client perspective or framed in terms of the company losing business in 2015. She also had admirable self-awareness that she was not going to be able to get the company there on her own. But the most important thing is that when push came to shove, faced with a binary choice—achieve your digital ambitions over-night, or move slowly and invest 100% of your profits in developing your people—she never even hesitated. She chose to invest in her people. While we continued the con-versation and haggled a little over the details, that was the moment I decided to join Lippe Taylor. It was just such a defining moment and so different from all the other agency founders I had met."

Okay, so how did we come together in practice? Paul likes to describe it as being very simple, and day by day, it was. Because of the approach we took, there wasn't the organizational whiplash that sometimes accompanies Rad-ical Reinvention.

Describing our approach, Paul says, "People always want a heuristic. Okay, are you like Edelman or McCann? When you try to say, oh no, we're something different, they say, I don't have time to figure this out. They want the easy heuristic. We didn't have the results though, or the case studies yet to prove that we were capable of meeting their expectations for another kind of agency. This is where I always say, 'When you can't pitch product, you pitch process.' So, we started talking about the process we were undertaking, and what it meant for our people and our clients. That's a critical part of this story. We're talking about Radical Reinvention, but we didn't go from *A* to *Z*, we went from *A* to *B* and *B* to *C*. In hindsight it appears radical, but in the moment each step felt natural. We started with a presentation of what our plan was and how we were going to develop our digital capabilities. It was six steps. We were not going to step three until we were excellent at two, because a lot of agencies had tried to leap and let people down. We wanted to maintain trust and reputation along the way. That means we couldn't go from being a well-respected PR firm with very little digital expertise and suddenly say, we're gonna build websites for the best brands in the world. We wouldn't be ready for that. We had to become great at social media first because it was a natural steppingstone. We spelled out the six steps and publicized it to hold ourselves accountable. We shared it with our staff. We shared it with some of our most trusted trade media leaders and with many clients. That was a moment of vulnerability saying, 'We're not great at this now, just give us some time and we won't disappoint.'"

Tough ride-or-die meetings ensued. For example, our client, a large skin care line, wanted everyone on the team to be digital experts. They were putting our feet to the fire and had called a meeting to see our plan. The woman who ran the entire business unit organized the meeting and preempted it by saying, "We appreciate the long partnership we've had with your agency. We like your people and believe that you're among the very best in the business at generating earned media results, getting key opinion leaders and celebrities contracted and on-message, and producing events that generate buzz. But our world is changing, and skin care is now a digital-first business. If you're not able to be that partner, we will need to reduce your scope to being only a media relations partner."

The implication of this was enormous. At $3M, this client was twenty percent of our entire business. The media relations scope was only a tenth of the overall budget ($300,000). I'm not sure how we would have weathered this storm without massively reducing headcount. Paul took the lead in preparing for the meeting and refused to let me see what he was preparing. We sat down together at the table, along with Lori Rubinson, and had the client and her head of marketing on the phone. At this point, I realized why Paul hadn't shown me the slides, because he was about to do something radical.

Paul opened the meeting by thanking them for their transparency and for giving us an opportunity to discuss their concerns. At this point, any other agency leader would start running through a list of digital capabilities, team members, freelancers, partners and vendors, case studies and promises. *Please, they would implore, just give us a chance, we will make this right!*

Instead, Paul had created a whole presentation and a grid of the services that he thought the client needed to succeed in the current digital landscape and some he projected they would need soon. Then he graded our own capabilities on a scale from, *1 to 10*. He was not favorable. In some areas we scored a *2 out of 10*. In others, we were a little better. I don't think we scored higher than 7 in anything. Then he went a step further and listed names of best-in-class agencies—our direct competitors, who were better than us in each of the services. Finally, he laid out our six-step plan, and talked them through where we were prioritizing, how we were investing, and what our timeline looked like. It was a massive bet.

When he had finished, the clients put the call on mute. That never happens! The few minutes that followed seemed like an eternity. Meanwhile, Paul, Lori, and I stared silently at each other. When the client returned, she opened with the most memorable response. "This was not what we expected, but it is what we needed. The truth is, we already knew this about you. We just needed to hear that you knew it, too. And that you have a plan in place. We value this partnership, and we will give you six months to do what you've laid out."

In other words, they loved it. They loved the transparency. They loved the honesty. They loved our ability to dive in deep to think about what we did best, but also where we were weak and how long it would take us to get stronger in areas that were priorities for them. With Paul's explanation of the process, rather than trying to sell them on our existing capabilities, they believed him.

"This is important to Radical Reinvention," Paul stresses. "You must be honest and know who you are because we've all seen it. Companies that suddenly shift with the tides saying, *Now, we're this!* No, just because you say something doesn't make it true."

Paul's honesty and transparency saved that client. It's still a major client today; in fact, it's nearly doubled in size, and we have their digital business as well. Thinking back, I'm not sure I took a breath in thirty minutes until the team came off mute and the client promised, "We will give you six months to do what you said you're going to do."

We got to work investing in new people and new tools. In six months, we went to Dallas and showed them all the results and implementation. It was enough time to prove that we were going through a Radical Reinvention for them, that we would prioritize them. They wanted us to succeed. They wanted us to win and step up to the plate. They didn't want to get rid of us. We knew their business inside out. I will say this about Paul's leadership: he brings total transparency. Even with our finances. Every month, our finance team takes the staff through our numbers, down to the penny. I was always so protective of that. Each team knew their budget, but they didn't know all in what we were worth. I saw the success of it. This is what people say on surveys: "You're so transparent and we so appreciate it." And in this marketplace, it goes a long way along with trust, respect, and honesty.

Paul adds: "At the five-year mark, people look back and say, the reinvention was successful, and we all feel so psyched about how far we've come. I know people think it was radical, but there was no whiplash. I came from an agency where there was whiplash, and it gutted the culture. Here, we've been moving along this continuum and communicated every step of the way. Here's where we are in the process. Here is what we're good at. Here's what we're *not* going to do. Most agencies don't follow this because they don't want to say no to a client. The reinvention has felt more like a natural evolution, but when you look in the rearview mirror, it looks like Radical Reinvention."

It was strategic, well-thought out and done with humanity. There were no surprises. Expectations of staff were clear. This is part of brand continuity—even as I am Radically Reinventing, I have held onto the core of who I am. That hasn't changed all the way back to day one. Even all these different iterations and situations. That is true about the company. We didn't stop being the "old" Lippe Taylor and start being a "different" Lippe Taylor. We held onto the core of our identity. We may talk about things a little differently. Like LVMH, we celebrate the traditional, as well as new capabilities. We've improved the core discipline while expanding it.

Enroll people in the reinvention right from the beginning and get their buy-in. Nobody does it by themselves. It doesn't matter if it's a whole company, brand or individual with their personal brand. Other people must believe it and support it. That's important in the good times and the challenging times.

When COVID-19 hit, the first month, we were still great. Two months later, our revenue plummeted. We were losing a million dollars a month. May through August. At our size, that was a significant amount. We were within a month or two of the bank account being empty. At the PR Council, calls were being held among agency owners and CEOs. *Cut*, they all said. *Cut now, or you'll regret it later*. Paul and I disagreed with that plan. If we had cut staff then, how could we have asked people to come back later? We got the whole company together in another moment of radical transparency. "Here's a list of every other agency announcing layoffs, pay cuts." A slide with a dozen headlines. Many of them were led by people on the calls with the PR Council. Our message to the staff was direct. "Our company is losing a million dollars a month. Everyone says we need to make cuts. If we cut you now, you're screwed because no one else will hire you." Then Paul put up a slideshow of recent work from the month of June. It was dazzling. "When I see work this good, I know it has to come back," he said. "So, we are not going to make cuts right now. No layoffs, no furloughs, no pay cuts. We are literally betting on you to beat the market." The team picked that up as a sort of rallying cry internally. "We're betting on us!" Consequently, the work that came out was innovative and award winning. That summer, they crushed it. We were quarantined at home and trying to keep each other sane with virtual happy hours, baking sourdough bread, sharing what we were streaming and just taking care of everybody with constant communication. We were coping just like the rest of the country and the world. We showed teams the numbers every month. They knew we had a short runway, but we were in it together.

Sometimes existential crises have a way of doing that. In a weak culture, they can break you, forcing everyone to look out for themselves. In a strong culture, they can bind you, bringing everyone together and enrolling them. "We must do something radical." Everything turned digital anyway. We weren't doing live events as you normally do in PR. Our growth went from 15 to 20 percent a year to 50 and 60 percent a year.

Trust inspired our people and cemented the reinvention. They knew conventional wisdom was that we should have cut our leadership team, cut staff, cut salaries. Paul had the guts to know it could pay off, however, and I totally believed in him and our great people. Those great people are still with us years later. We're proud to report that to you. That's what matters. We survived together.

Paul says, "Our retention rate through the great resignation was over 90 percent. *PRWeek* said the industry turnover rate was 30-40 percent turnover and ours was less than 10 percent. I believe in a few things: A company can't ask for an employee to be loyal if the company isn't also loyal. That doesn't mean loyalty is endless and people can get away with not being accountable. Still, that old adage of 'hire slow and fire fast' is tired and outdated. People shouldn't lose their job when things get tough, if the company can sustain. The company should have high expectations of people, but also try hard to be loyal to its people. And we were. Like Maureen agreeing to invest all her profit in training people new skills. We spent millions of dollars demonstrating our loyalty during lockdown. I also believe the company should be a community. Too many companies have tried to push the disingenuous notion that the company is a 'family'. That's what cults do! Our company is a community of people who respect and care for each other. We are there for each other, and we celebrate achievements, stories and milestones that are both professional and personal. But everyone who works here has their own family. Those families come first. When you think of Radical Reinvention, the lionized examples are often people sacrificing everything for tech startups, places like the Apple or Theranos cults. It doesn't have to be like that. You can be part of a community that plays a really important role in your life without needing to put it above your own family.

"Another point is the influence of the rest of the leadership team in this kind of reinvention. It's the yin and yang between different members of the leadership team. For *radical*, you tend to think of the new in your mind and it becomes a consuming thought, but you have clients paying you for work you've been delivering for a long time now. You also have people whose self-worth is wrapped up in what they've been doing. They have understandable fears. If the company reinvents itself, am I only valuable if I change? Are the new people more valuable than me? We purposefully alternated between the voice of *what's next* and being the comforting voice of, *we still value you*.

"As with most trends, COVID-19 was an accelerator. It didn't create new trends for us. It accelerated more digital presence in clients. A crisis can drive people apart or bring them together. In some agencies, the leadership teams disappeared and focused on their individual lives. They were too panicked to be there for others or didn't know what employees expected. Some did the opposite, clamping down and trying to micromanage everything. We did our best to reinforce our values, support our people, and bring them together with the right amount of transparency, communication, and connection. Doing so accelerated our reinvention."

So, what comes next? We continue reinventing. Paul exemplified this recently by talking openly in an all-staff meeting about how it was time to shake off the defensive posture we all adopted during the pandemic and re-commit ourselves to a culture of growth. On the surface this sounds obvious. Everybody wants to grow. It's not hard to get them to buy into the idea of personal and career growth, plus they love the excitement of seeing their clients and company grow as well. However, especially given the trends of the day with mental health concerns and employees being empowered to demand whatever they wanted from employers; it was challenging to push them like we used to. While some leaders may have shied away from this aspect of the conversation, Paul addressed it head-on with characteristic transparency. Wanting both personal growth and constant comfort to coexist was paradoxical, he told the staff. If you want to grow, embrace being uncomfortable. He was careful to draw a distinction between this and *hustle culture*. It's not about working hard for the sake of it. It's about redefining your goals to be about growth rather than daily comfort or satisfaction. He gave a whole presentation about the benefits of being uncomfortable. By doing things you haven't done before. By seeking out the negative feedback. He used the example of employees who would say things like, "I'm open to negative feedback, but I need praise to stay motivated…" Those people never grew as quickly as the ones who deliberately sought out feedback about what they could do better. It was imperative that everyone saw this challenge of embracing being uncomfortable as an opportunity to grow, as something that could make them better.

Six years after Paul and I started this process of reinvention, Lippe Taylor has grown tremendously in annual fees. During a pandemic! No other independent agency posted as much organic growth in that time. Our employee retention is still among the highest in the industry, and our clients stay with us for just as long. Along the way, we've produced some of the most-awarded work in recent memory while being named the agency of the year several times. ...And we've had a blast doing it. Radical!

BARRI RAFFERTY: BANKING ON PR SKILLS

FORMER KETCHUM **CEO,** an Omnicom Group agency, and top woman in PR, Barri Rafferty steered into a radical turn to join Wells Fargo in July 2020 as head of corporate communications. She took an agency through going remote at the start of COVID-19, then accepted the pressure-laden job at Wells Fargo where she didn't meet anyone in-person for eight months and redesigned a department in the middle of all that. It's hard to describe the intensity of those two years, but Barri is also my good friend, and I am radically proud of all that she has achieved. The wisdom she shares here about rebranding is far-reaching.

Relationships and trust have no substitute.

Wells Fargo employs 250,000 employees, and I was responsible for all communications. I didn't meet my team for a year, but we figured out how to build relationships and trust through a combo of calls, Zoom, emails and texting. In challenging times, you realize who you can trust and bond with, and technology was an incredible enabler. You had to have a combination of intuition and reading business cues, combining them in a different way. When I arrived, my department had 500 people and one of my first tasks was to reimagine and redress how it functioned. My team worked to redesign how we created content, streamlined roles, and attracted new talent. I created new jobs and new ways of working. Over-communicating is critical to get buy-in for change. People told me I created a lot of optimism, which is a feature of my personality. I remained consistent, empathetic and a coach, day in and day out.

You can change culture if you are up to the task.

Banks are enormous businesses and like all enormous businesses, the legal department is often the tail that wags the dog. Three weeks into my position at Wells Fargo, there was a negative story about to break on national television that would have really put the company in a bad light. A response team was quickly assembled and on one of our strategy calls there were thirteen people: seven of them lawyers plus scattered representation from communicators and brand management. Obviously, it was the legal department leading how we should respond and what language we should use. The non-lawyers simply accepted legal's position.

Unfortunately, legal's response would have been the

wrong one. "We're not giving this quote to the network," I said. "I need one lawyer and one person on my team to get off this call and work on this together, and we're going to sound like we really care about these people." Except for one senior manager who offered to help, no one else said a word, because culturally, no one ever pushed back on legal's language.

Within hours, and with legal support, we created a very consumer-friendly statement and circulated it to the network that night. It became a corporate cultural turning point, becoming more publicly empathetic. Legal became a strong partner over time, collaborating with the communications and marketing teams.

Imagine your impact.

As you reimagine and go into new places, you bring fresh perspective as a change agent. The PR trades were shocked when I left a top agency job to go corporate. But when you think about reimagining, I had done everything in the PR agency world and could still do this well for ten more years. But as an avid learner, I thought, *what else am I going to learn and how can I best apply it?* There was something about going in-house that said, "I can run a large department and get back to the craft of what I'd started out doing—communications, branding, strategy"—versus my CEO role at Ketchum, focusing on new business and never seeing the transformation of existing clients the same way as a client director. Some of it was a big change and very different, but it also allowed me to leverage everything I had learned throughout my career to date.

Every new job is a chance to reinvent yourself.

Two important questions in business are: What do I want to be known for? What do I want to leave behind? I consider this with every new opportunity. Every agency promotion, every move, first to Atlanta then back to New York City, I had a chance to reset my leadership style. Then the Wells Fargo opportunity gave me a chance to stretch myself even further in a new industry.

I did ten interviews with Wells Fargo via Zoom, some of which were with operations committee members sharing their values and their goal to modernize the department. Even though I did not have deep banking expertise, I knew I could lean in and bring differentiation with the diverse client expertise and management skills I had honed. What helped close the deal for me though was the opportunity to work with Bill Daley, who had served as President Obama's chief of staff for a year. Over the course of three virtual meetings, I knew I could learn from Bill and joined in order to partner with him to modernize and transform the department.

It's hard to be everything to everybody when you start something new, so you must prioritize and be true to your personal brand, while being open to reinvention. Where and how you spend your energy and capital is critical to how you are perceived. Before Wells Fargo, I was seen as an empathetic leader. Now I needed to marry that with the ability to show up for meetings and deliver tougher messages in tougher situations.

If you're not curious, you can't reinvent.

Always have a reporter mentality. When I joined, we were in a defensive bunker not telling our story. Issues of the day prevailed and sucked the energy of the team. A huge part of our reinvention was getting on the front foot and executing a strategic communications plan. I told my team after a particularly bad news cycle, "We're going out with this launch, and we will not veer from our forward momentum. We will be undaunted." Even on my last week, I would not let up and kept the team focused on delivering. What I learned from Bill is to always project calm. Everyone would be freaking out, but he handled issue after issue and reset every day. This shared attitude was huge for the strength needed to keep us on track. It helped us to begin to move the needle on trust and favorability, and gain confidence that taking a new approach would pay off.

Keep up your courage.

Bill encouraged me by saying, "We need someone like you who will bring outside perspective." It was a good partnership. Having someone you know has your back is important. I wouldn't be successful at this kind of transformation without allies, helping me make necessary changes in both the agency and a large corporation. You need a lot of personal confidence, which is also reinforced by having others in your corner. I built a strong team internally, developed relationships throughout the company and surrounded myself with a personal advisory board. You need others to be that inner voice for you. With your friends and family and within your work realm, you must find those people who will be honest with you.

Stretch yourself to get past discomfort and to make incremental change. How do you continue to build that strength? Try new things and don't be intimidated. COVID-19 changed so many people and required them to lean on technology that they were not immediately comfortable with. It created stress, but also strengthened a lot of people in ways they never expected. For years, I have relied on my IT department when it comes to technology. But when starting a new job at home during a pandemic and receiving boxes of high tech from Wells Fargo, my initial panic thankfully gave way to me building confidence as I conquered a setup my teenage child could have done in half the time. Relying on muscle memory to get the job done boosted my confidence and emboldened me.

Practice calm in the crazy.

Find what grounds you. I've gotten into yoga, and I get up and give myself time to stretch and go outdoors to clear my head. It's important to find outlets because the world is just stressful. Harness the ability to rebound and identify what will allow you to reset, what will reenergize you.

Reflection on Barri's Radical Reinvention

Barri entered the new territory of a very different industry amidst the pandemic and quarantine. What a radical learning curve! But my friend balanced her existing skill set of openness, curiosity, and confidence, all the personality traits that had previously landed her the prestigious position of CEO of a top global PR firm, with experimentation, imagination, emotional intelligence, and stellar communication. Going to the corporate side was brave, courageous and a major stretch for Barri which she conquered with empathetic leadership in a company not used to that kind of culture. She was not happy with the status quo—she helped to improve policies amidst complicating circumstances and stood for what she wanted to be known for, leaving those imprints on a massive brand, their employees, and their clients. Never forget what you want to be known for. What's your WHY?

MY RADICAL CONCLUSION

I STARTED TO write this book to help myself reinvent, as well as for you, from a state of emptiness after losing my greatest love. The process supported my recovery. It was my therapy; it was my therapist. Soon, though, this two-year journey took on a life of its own. I tried someone else's tools, invented my own tools, fell hard and then scraped myself off, trying on new shades of self-image, self-discovery, self-invention (and yes, self-bashing at times). I learned to sleep peacefully again and reawaken with some semblance of joy, right down to smelling the roses just a little longer—the magic is in the *moments*! I have forged ahead with new memories, as the old ones can sometimes be crippling, bringing back the loneliness for the one man who took my breath away for almost forty years.

I got back in touch with parts of myself that had formed in my childhood, particularly the love of my family. I reviewed my glorious magazine editorial career, stopping to acknowledge all the steps, role models, advisors, influences and even failures. I forged an even greater and deeper relationship with my son, Nick, through letting him see and feel my pain and loneliness, but also letting him witness firsthand, my strength and need to authentically heal myself my way with intention, but without depending on anyone else. We together shared our pain of losing the most important man in our lives. I discovered new things about myself and the world. I learned to remember all that I love about my beloved husband, smile, and move forward to the next minutes without succumbing to feelings of emptiness or anxiety. Honestly, I also went through this process for him, as the fearless, confident, risk-taking woman he fell in love with. I continue to strive for happiness over anger or sympathy. I'm trying my best and my way. It's still a process that sometimes sneaks up on me with profound sadness, but it departs quickly now. That sadness is like an old friend who calls on me from time to time. It used to be all day, every day. My gratitude for the whole healing process is indescribable. It's almost as if I didn't know ME. I know ME better now. I found my courage and I put it to work, and it was hard work. I now know I can do really hard things. I also kept my humor most of the time, as it lightened my heart and was my pathway to peace. I am also grateful to have been working at Lippe Taylor during this process of healing; it was my true lifeline. It was my connection to my community of colleagues and friends who are part of my family and a big part of my recovery and survival.

When I look at the cover of this book featuring our beloved turtle now, with wheels, I see myself. It says to me, you will get there! You're now moving forward faster, and that's all you can ask of yourself. My hope is that all my courageous Re-Inventors who you have met in this book will help you harness their insights—and let's move forward together down the Radical Reinvention Road. Embrace the future you have longed for most of your life. There has never been a better time than now for reinvention to develop your potential and purpose. Test your courage and rise again.

There is not a more powerful analogy than starting the Radical Reinvention at rock bottom, or "on the floor", as Keiya Rayne graciously taught us. So many of you already relate to that 3:00 a.m. scene she described from her own life. Our Re-Inventors kept me going! Their willingness to share and empathize was so filled with honesty and humanity. Literally in the hours when I was not motivated to review, remember, feel, process, I thought of their stories—what they endured and how they transformed. Sharing my story and our Re-Inventors' stories with the world became my mission and purpose to help me and help others get up, be brave, be proud and have confidence we are all moving closer to the light both personally and professionally. I couldn't finish this book, the process of going down the Radical Reinvention Road, without my trusted Re-Inventors. They were my salvation to not only navigate the journey of recovery, but also, enjoy the rewards of renewal.

Whether you are a serial re-inventor like me or a first timer, I so hope that our stories and reinvention toolbox have helped you not only survive, but also, get your wheels back on to fly with glorious movement, reinvention, and joy to thrive, just like our trusted turtle.

REFERENCES

Interviews

Eric Alva, Zoom, May 26, 2022
Liza Andrews, In person, January 16, 2022
Elizabeth G. Bailey, Zoom, June 24, 2022
Irene Brank, Zoom, April 7, 2022
Weatherly Camacho, Phone, April 18, 2022
Halena Cline, In person, September 21, 2022
Paul Dyer, Zoom, April 14, 2022
Alina Lee, Zoom, May 9, 2022
Samantha Lux, Phone, May 12, 2022
Fern Mallis, Zoom, June 23, 2022
Barri Rafferty, Zoom, May 3, 2022
Keiya Rayne, In person, April 21, 2023
Irina Soriano, Zoom, May 26, 2022
Craig Stanland, Zoom, April 18, 2022
Nick Taylor, Zoom, April 26, 2022
Ann Turner, Zoom, May 26, 2022
Carlos Zepeda, Zoom, June 17, 2022
Nadya Zhexembayeva, Zoom, April 19, 2022

Publications

Ampoloquio, Ray. "Producer describes next 007 film as a "reinvention of Bond." *xFire*. July 18, 2022.

https://www.xfire.com/
producer-next-007-film-reinvention-of-bond/

Andrews, Liza.
http://www.lizaandrews.com

Beer, Jeff. "The Great American Rebrand." *Fast Company.* November 16, 2020.
https://www.fastcompany.com/90569630/
the-great-american-rebrand

Brady, Susan MacKenty. *Mastering Your Inner Critic and 7 Other High Hurdles to Advancement: How the Best Women Leaders Practice Self-Awareness to Change What Really Matters.* New York, New York: McGraw-Hill Professional, November 29, 2018.

Brower, Tracy. "Science Proves the Power of Nature: 3 Ways to Improve Work and Life." *Forbes.* April 14, 2022.
https://www.forbes.com/sites/tracybrower/2022/08/14/
science-proves-the-power-of-nature-3-ways-to-improve-work-
and-life/?sh=469447c13469

Clinton, Michael. *Roar: into the second half of your life (before it's too late).* Atria Books/Beyond Words. September 7, 2021.

Dyer, Paul. *Friction Fatigue: What the Failure of Advertising Means for Future-Focused Brands.* New York, New York: Author's Republic, May 21, 2021.

Free, Cathy. "The world's oldest living land animal? At age 190, it's Jonathan the tortoise." *The Washington Post.* January 30, 2022.
https://www.washingtonpost.com/lifestyle/2022/01/31/
oldest-animal-tortoise-jonathan-/

Gorjestani, Kethevane, and Fanny Allard. "What are the reasons behind the 'Great Resignation' in the US?" *France24.* January 28, 2022.
https://www.france24.com/en/tv-shows/reporters/20220128-
what-are-the-reasons-behind-the-great-resignation-in-the-us

Horowitz, Ben. *The Hard Thing About Hard Things: Building a*

Business When There Are No Easy Answers. New York, New York: Harper Business. March 4, 2014.

Kane, Brendan. *Hook Point.* Cardiff, California: Waterside Productions. September 29, 2020.

Kessler, David. *Finding Meaning: The Sixth Stage of Grief.* New York, New York: Simon and Schuster, September 1, 2020.

Markson, Mitch. *The Imagination Playbook: For People, Brands, Issues, and Organizations.* New York, New York: Markson Ideacraft. February 2020.

Morin, Monte. "How the turtle got its shell." *Los Angeles Times.* May 31, 2013.
https://www.latimes.com/science/la-xpm-2013-may-31-la-sci-sn-how-the-turtle-got-its-shell-20130530-story.html

Mukherjee, Rashmi Bhaskar, Ashok Krish. "5 ways the COVID-19 pandemic is changing the role of leaders." World Economic Forum. October 4, 2021.
https://www.weforum.org/agenda/2021/10/5-ways-the-pandemic-is-changing-the-role-of-leaders/

Shirin, Ali. "The pandemic weighs heavy on the minds of Gen Z." *The Hill.* December 7, 2021.
https://thehill.com/changing-america/well-being/mental-health/584786-the-pandemic-weighs-heavy-on-the-minds-of-gen-z

Susskind, Daniel, James Manyika, Jean Saldahna, Sharan Burrow, Sergio Rebelo, and Ian Bremmer. "Six prominent thinkers reflect on how the pandemic has changed the world." *International Monetary Fund,* June 2020.
https://www.imf.org/Publications/fandd/issues/2020/06/how-will-the-world-be-different-after-COVID-19.

ABOUT THE AUTHOR

Maureen Lippe is founder and chairman of Lippe Taylor. Over the course of 30 years, Maureen has provided brand-building counsel to leading companies including Procter & Gamble, Bayer, Walmart, Clairol, Constellation Brands, IKEA, Johnson & Johnson, Allergan, Nestle, Keurig Dr. Pepper, Intel, Kmart, and Nordstrom. Maureen began her career as a fashion editor at *Vogue* magazine and then served as beauty and health editor at *Harper's Bazaar*.

Maureen has worked with organizations such as Save The Children, UNICEF, Look Good / Feel Better, Women in Need and the Step Up Network for Girls. She has been honored by the United Cerebral Palsy Foundation as a "Woman Who Cares" and was the only non-physician member of the Skin Cancer Foundation board. She also spearheaded IKEA's "Soft Toys for Education" partnership with UNICEF and Save the Children, which reached a million disadvantaged children in 17 different countries.

Radical Reinvention is her debut book.